The 500 Hidden Secrets of
LOS ANGELES

D1293572

INTRODUCTION

'In Los Angeles, all of us travel in undiscovered countries.'
– D. J. Waldie, *Where We Are Now: Notes from Los Angeles*

There's no pithy way to sum up Los Angeles – not just because it's enormous, but because of the city's changing character. Los Angeles is a multifaceted place with a dynamic history that can't be easily reduced. And that's the way we like it.

Los Angeles is also a mythic place. So much of what we know about the city comes from cinema, literature, music, and TV. There's the glossy vision of what LA is and then there's the dark noir – both are fictions. First-time visitors are often startled at the fissure between the imaginary and the real. This hazy space of half-truths and real make-believe is as enchanting as the marine layer that sometimes descends over the city, obscuring the obvious landmarks. There are so many sides to LA; so many stories still untold.

The only qualification for initiation into *The 500 Hidden Secrets of Los Angeles* is curiosity. We hope this highly subjective book surprises you. The author hopes it's expansive in the same way that living here is. There's so much to do and see beyond the usual narrative of LA, so put on some comfortable shoes and stylish sunglasses (that's one cliché that sticks), because it's time to explore.

HOW TO USE THIS BOOK?

This guide lists 500 things you need to know about Los Angeles in 100 different categories. Most of these are places to visit, with practical information to help you find your way. Others are bits of information that help you get to know the city and its habitants. The aim of this guide is to inspire, not to cover the city from A to Z.

The places listed in the guide are given an address, including the neighborhood (for example Venice or West Hollywood), and a number. The neighborhood and number allow you to find the locations on the maps at the beginning of the book: first look for the map of the corresponding neighborhood, then look for the right number. A word of caution however: these maps are not detailed enough to allow you to find specific locations in the city. You can obtain an excellent map from any tourist office or in most hotels. Or the addresses can be located on a smartphone.

Please also bear in mind that cities change all the time. The chef who hits a high note one day may be uninspiring on the day you happen to visit. The hotel ecstatically reviewed in this book might suddenly go downhill under a new manager. The bar considered one of the best cocktail bars might be empty on the night you visit. This is obviously a highly personal selection. You might not always agree with it. If you want to leave a comment, recommend a bar or reveal your favorite secret place, please visit the website *www.the500hiddensecrets.com* – you'll also find free tips and the latest news about the series there – or follow *@500hiddensecrets* on Instagram or Facebook and leave a comment.

THE AUTHOR

Andrea Richards is a contributing writer to *Los Angeles* magazine and the author of *Girl Director: A How-To Guide for the First-Time, Flat-Broke Film and Video Maker* and *Los Angeles Cocktails: Spirits in the City of Angels*. She is part of the LA-based publishing collective Narrated Objects and the coeditor of its book, *We Heart P-22: A Coloring + Activity Book Celebrating L.A.'s Most Famous Mountain Lion*. She is proud to live in Silver Lake, the neighborhood just down the road from that mountain lion's home in Griffith Park.

After twenty (lucky) years of living in LA, the author has many people to thank, folks who have shared their own favorite bits of the city along the way: first and foremost her collaborator, Giovanni Simeone, who shot the beautiful photographs in this book and first introduced her to Luster. Andrea thanks all at Luster, including the patient and kind editor Dettie Luyten, who made working on this book a pleasure.

Andrea also owes so much to her friends and colleagues in LA who have delighted in exploring it with her (in words and in adventures), especially Teena Apeles, Jessica Hoffmann, and Nina Wiener – all native Angelenos! Mentors and friends Paddy Calistro, Scott McAuley, and Amy Inouye of Angel City Press first introduced Andrea to unsung aspects of the city's history and have been cultivating her interests in it ever since. Friend and writing coach Maia Danziger always encourages Andrea, as does agent and enthusiast Betsy Amster; she thanks both for their ongoing support. Andrea is also grateful to her former editors at *Los Angeles* magazine, including Ann Herold, Mary Melton, Kit Rachlis, and Amy Wallace, who allowed her to write stories about the city, from pest control to tanning trends. Also, a few of the places in this book were discovered thanks to Aaron Paley, who hired Andrea to write neighborhood guides for CicLAvia and is one of the city's greatest proponents of public space.

And finally Andrea offers much gratitude to her family for their ongoing support, including her extended family in North Carolina and elsewhere; her sister, Kara, and Drew and the boys; her parents, Eileen and Jerry Richards, who (perhaps inadvertently) inspired Andrea's wanderlust with their own adventures; her husband, Norwood Cheek, who first led Andrea to LA (although she'd never admit that at the time); and their two daughters, Phoebe and Gray, who have the good fortune of growing up in this wonderful city. May its future be as bright as they are!

LOS ANGELES

overview

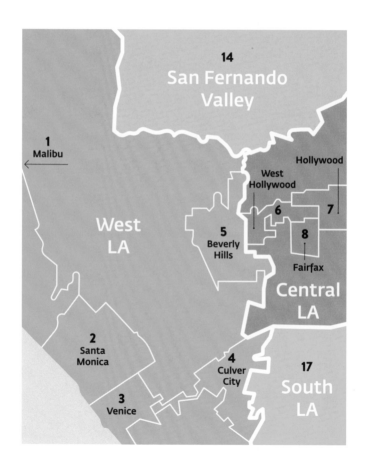

14
San Fernando Valley

1
Malibu

Hollywood

West Hollywood

West LA

6

7

5
Beverly Hills

8

Fairfax

Central LA

2
Santa Monica

4
Culver City

17
South LA

3
Venice

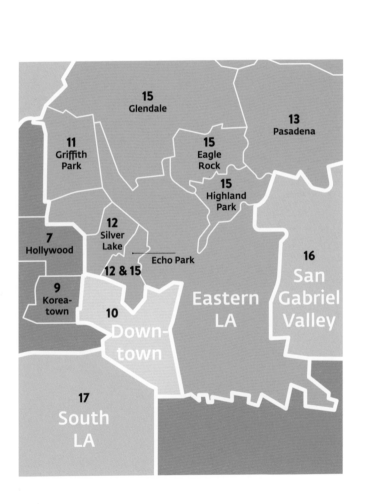

WEST LA
overview

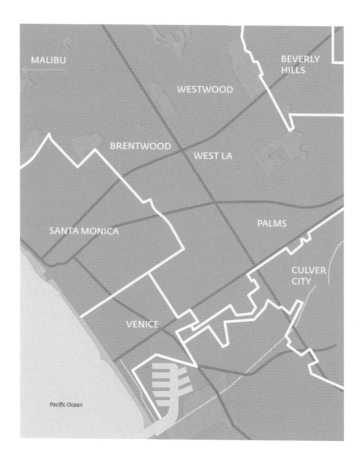

MALIBU ←

BEVERLY HILLS

WESTWOOD

BRENTWOOD

WEST LA

SANTA MONICA

PALMS

CULVER CITY

VENICE

Pacific Ocean

Map 1
MALIBU

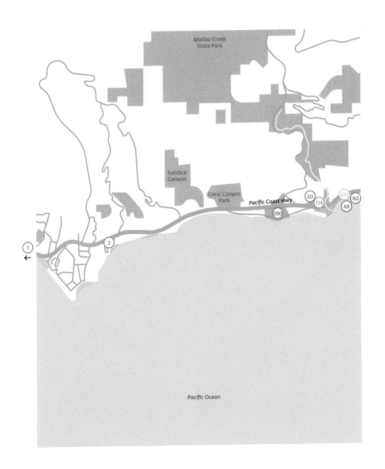

Map 2
SANTA MONICA

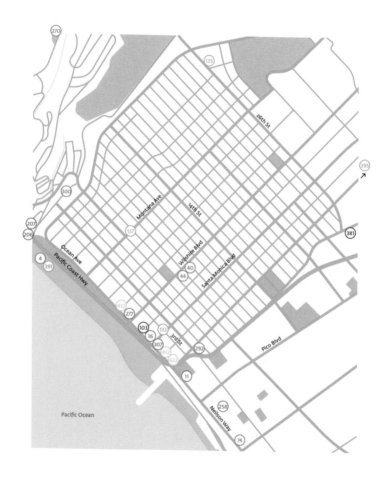

Map 3
VENICE

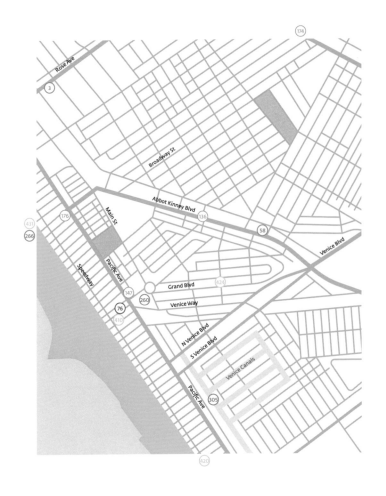

Map 4
CULVER CITY

Map 5
BEVERLY HILLS

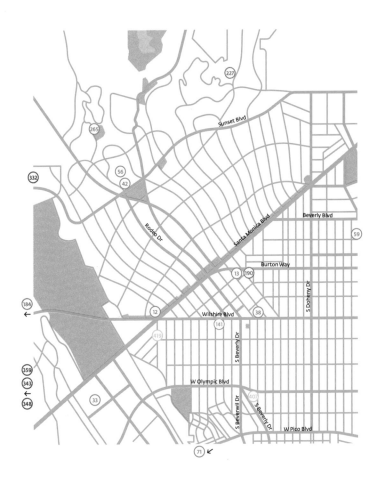

CENTRAL LA
overview

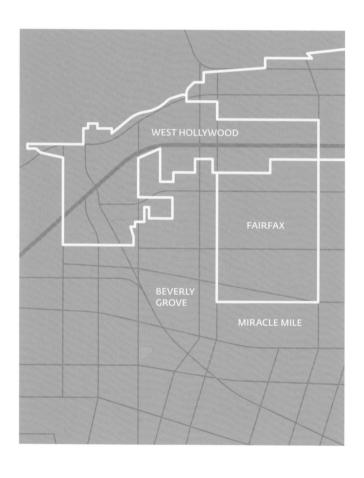

WEST HOLLYWOOD

FAIRFAX

BEVERLY
GROVE

MIRACLE MILE

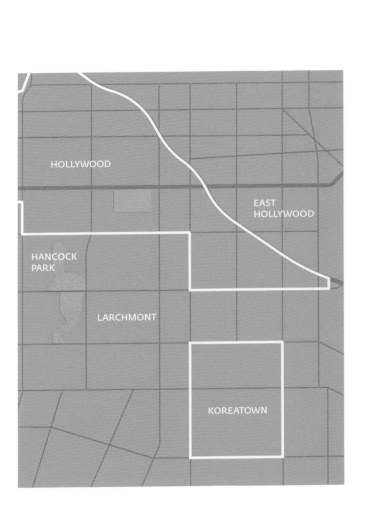

Map 6
WEST HOLLYWOOD

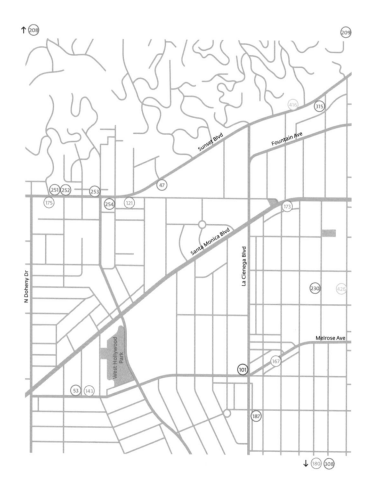

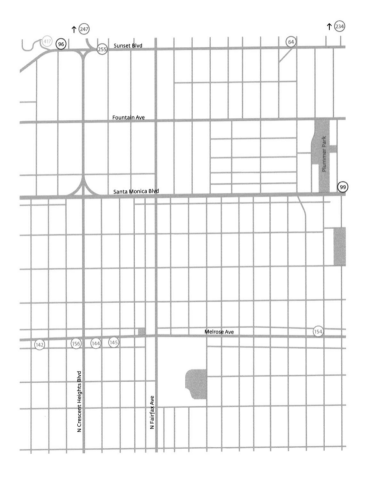

Map 7
HOLLYWOOD

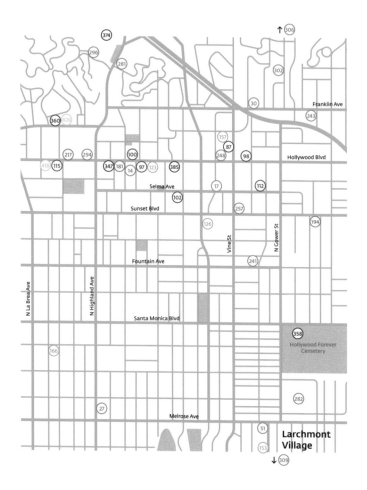

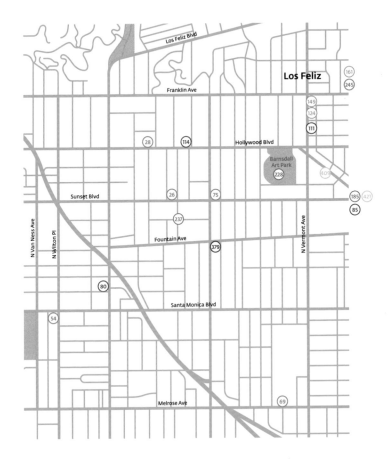

Map 8
FAIRFAX

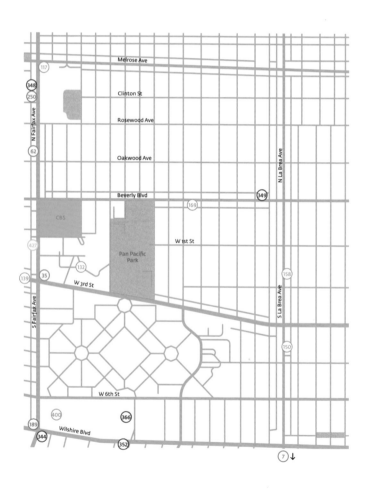

Map 9
KOREATOWN

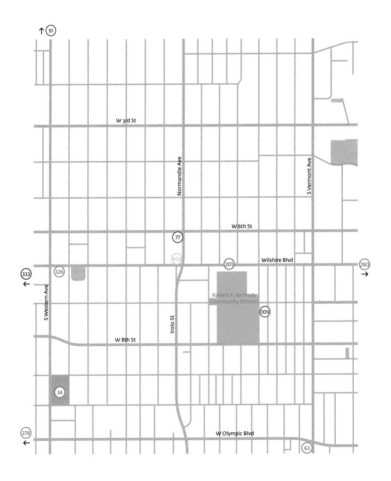

Map 10
DOWNTOWN

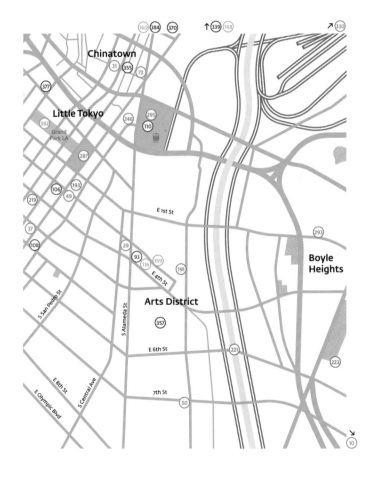

EASTERN LA
overview

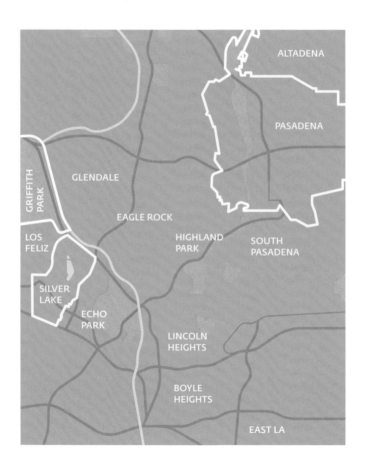

ALTADENA

PASADENA

GLENDALE

GRIFFITH PARK

EAGLE ROCK

LOS FELIZ

HIGHLAND PARK

SOUTH PASADENA

SILVER LAKE

ECHO PARK

LINCOLN HEIGHTS

BOYLE HEIGHTS

EAST LA

Map 11
GRIFFITH PARK

Map 12
SILVER LAKE
and ECHO PARK

Map 13
PASADENA

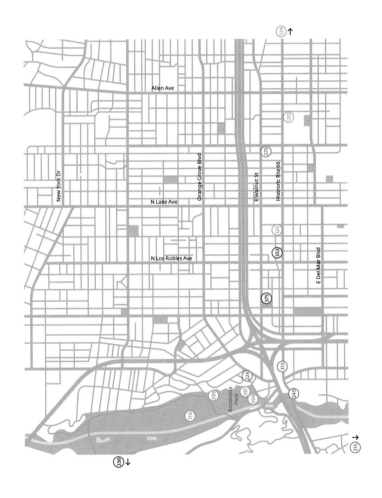

Allen Ave

New York Dr

Orange Grove Blvd

N Lake Ave

E Walnut St

Historic Rte 66

N Los Robles Ave

E Del Mar Blvd

Brookside Park

Map 14
SAN FERNANDO
VALLEY

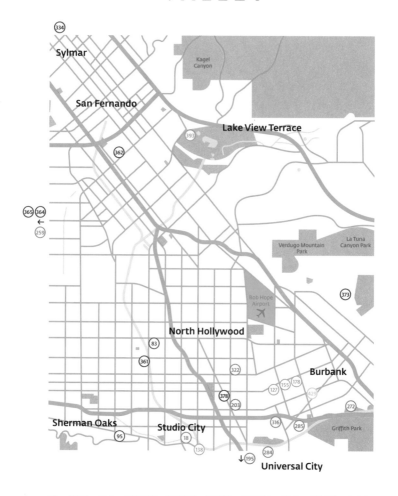

Map 15

GLENDALE, EAGLE ROCK,
ECHO PARK and HIGHLAND PARK

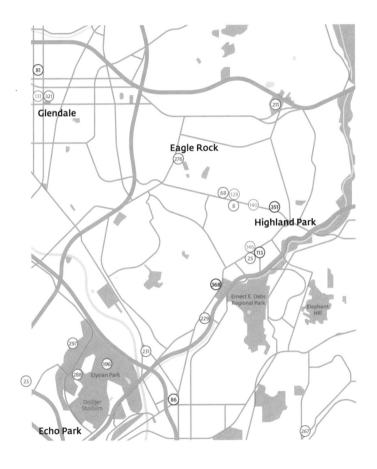

Map 16
SAN GABRIEL VALLEY

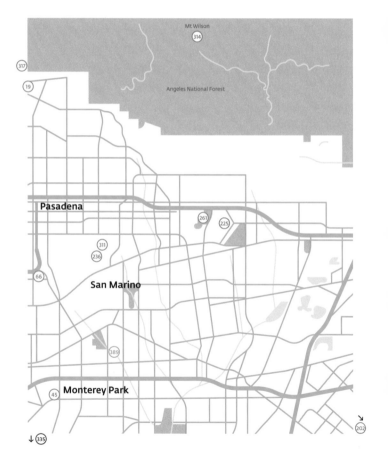

Map 17
SOUTH OF LA

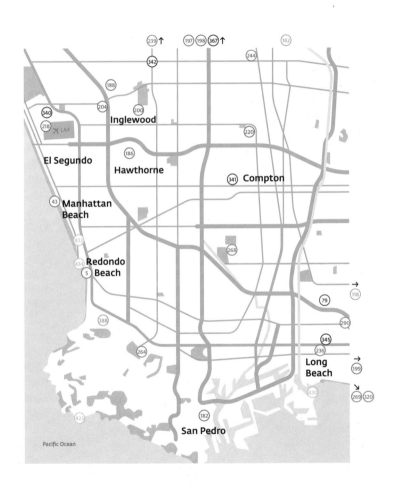

239 ↑   197 198 367 ↑   162

342

244

188

340   204   200
        Inglewood
218 ✈ LAX   220

El Segundo   186
              Hawthorne   341 Compton

43 Manhattan
   Beach

433
                                  268

434 Redondo
5   Beach
                                              →
                                              118

                                         79

                                              →
388   290

                                         345
       264   236
                                         Long
                                         Beach   →
                                                  199

                                         430   ↘
                                                  269 320

                  421

                       182
Pacific Ocean   San Pedro

NOBU MALIBU

75 PLACES TO EAT OR BUY GOOD FOOD

———

5 laidback
BEACH CAFES

---

1   NEPTUNE'S NET

42505 Pacific Coast
Highway
Malibu ①
+1 310 457 3095
neptunesnet.com

Located at the tip of Los Angeles County,
this local landmark might be the world's
most perfect seafood shack, offering fresh
catch, great views, and a mix of surfers,
bikers, and tourists. Open since 1956,
Neptune's Net captures the SoCal vibe
so well it's no surprise the spot is
a frequent film location.

2   PARADISE COVE BEACH CAFÉ

28128 Pacific Coast
Highway
Malibu ①
+1 310 457 2503
*paradisecove
malibu.com*

Another historic and unpretentious
beach cafe serving seafood and American
fare. The food here is second to the
atmosphere – patrons at the cafe gain
access to a gorgeous private beach,
so plan to make an afternoon out of it.
There are beds and lounges for rent,
ideal for siesta or watching the sunset.

3   THE ROSE CAFÉ

220 Rose Avenue
Venice ③
+1 310 399 0711
rosecafevenice.com

Opened in 1979, this iconic Venice cafe
is so beloved that when it closed for
a brief time, the entire city bemoaned
the loss. Now it's back with market-driven
SoCal cuisine – breakfast, lunch, dinner,
coffee, cocktails, and pastries – that can
be enjoyed indoors or out.

4 **BACK ON THE BEACH CAFÉ**
445 Pacific Coast Highway
Santa Monica ②
+1 310 393 8282
backonthebeach cafe.com

Built on the site of the former Marion Davies estate, the Annenberg Community Beach House spans five acres of beachfront and offers parking reservations, a beautiful beach, and a pool. The best part of the cafe is that you don't have to leave to eat; simply enjoy seasonal cuisine with your feet in the sand.

5 **TONY'S ON THE PIER**
210 Fisherman's Wharf
Redondo Beach ⑰
+1 310 374 1442
oldtonys.com

Family-owned and -operated since 1952, Old Tony's, as it's called, is named after its founder, a former fisherman and local legend. You can't get closer to the water than this, and along with the great history and ambiance the restaurant has a second-story bar with a view from Palos Verdes to Santa Monica.

5 TONY'S ON THE PIER

5
TACO TRUCKS
you must try

---

6 KOGI
VARIOUS LOCATIONS
AT: KOGI TAQUERIA
3500 Overland
Avenue #100
Palms ④
+1 424 326 3031
kogibbq.com

This truck launched the trend for hip food trucks and unexpected street fusion food. Before he became world-famous, Chef Roy Choi perfected Kogi's Korean tacos, which are now emblems of the city itself – and much easier to come by thanks to expansion (four trucks now and two brick-and-mortars).

7 TACOS LEO
1515 S La Brea Ave
Mid City ⑧
+1 323 346 2001
leostacotruck.com

There is often a long line, late into the night, in the gas station parking lot where this truck is parked. The crowds are here for one thing: *al pastor,* marinated pork cooked vertically on a spit that is thin-cut and served on tortillas as tacos.

8 TACOS LA ESTRELLA
5319 York Boulevard
& Avenue 54
Highland Park ⑮

In a city of so many fine tacos, sometimes what stands out is simplicity. La Estrella's *carne asada tacos* are straightforward: smoky meat, onion, cilantro, salsa roja. Plus, unlike most that roam nocturnally through the city streets, this truck is permanent (no chasing them down on Twitter) and open during the day.

9 RICKY'S FISH TACOS

3201 Riverside Drive
Los Feliz ⑪

A Baja fish taco done right is a thing of beauty and Ricky Piña, a Baja native, is the master. The accolades for this truck are many but who cares about awards? Instead enjoy the most delicious lunch you can find for less than five dollars: expertly fried fish or shrimp with homemade salsas and aqua frescas.

10 MARISCOS JALISCO

3040 E Olympic
Boulevard
Boyle Heights ⑩
+1 323 528 6701

Here is another taco that tops every serious foodie's list: the *taco dorado de camaron,* which are deep-fried shrimp tacos topped with avocado and salsa roja. Several other trucks in the neighborhood offer similar tacos, but go for the one most critics deem best. Or try a ceviche, also delicious.

8 TACOS LA ESTRELLA

5

RAT PACK ERA

restaurants

---

11 CHEZ JAY

1657 Ocean Avenue
Santa Monica ②
+1 310 395 1741
chezjays.com

A favorite of celebrities since it opened in 1959, this diminutive steak-and-seafood joint was named in homage to Chez Joey, a restaurant in a Frank Sinatra film. In a case of life imitating art, Sinatra and the rest of the gang were frequent customers taking table #10.

12 LA DOLCE VITA

9785 Santa Monica
Boulevard
Beverly Hills ⑤
+1 310 278 1845
*ladolcevita
beverlyhills.com*

This throwback Northern Italian restaurant is where Sinatra often enjoyed the Veal Milanese and Rigatoni Pomodoro; when he was with his fourth wife, Barbara, he drank wine; with his rat pack pals, it was Jack Daniels. Today, the 50-year-old landmark has a booth dedicated to Ol' Blue Eyes.

13 LA SCALA

434 N Canon Drive
Beverly Hills ⑤
+1 310 275 0579
lascalabeverlyhills.com

Serving Hollywood stars and moguls (founder Jean Leon delivered Marilyn Monroe's last meal) since 1956, this is another swanky, red-booth Italian joint. But the focus is not on the pasta or the well-known patrons – the most famous thing here is the chopped salad.

14 MICELI'S

1646 N Las Palmas
Avenue
Hollywood ⑦
+1 323 466 3438
micelisrestaurant.com

When Carmen Miceli opened in 1949, he sold 35-cent pizza. While the pie is more these days, his namesake restaurant retains its old-school charm. Sinatra, Dean Martin, Joe DiMaggio, Marilyn Monroe, and Elizabeth Taylor are just a few of the famous to patronize the place, along with presidents Kennedy and Nixon.

15 MATTEO'S

2321 Westwood Blvd
Westwood ④
+1 310 475 4521
matteosla.com

The original owner of this swank red-sauce joint grew up across the street from Sinatra in Hoboken, New Jersey. A corner booth was always reserved for his famous friend, and the rich and famous continue to frequent the place. It's rumored that Muhammad Ali once performed magic tricks at the bar.

5
FARMERS' MARKETS
not to miss

---

16 SANTA MONICA DOWNTOWN FARMERS' MARKET

Arizona Avenue
(at 2nd St)
Santa Monica ②
+1 310 458 8712
smgov.net

With the temperate weather and endless sunshine, LA has incredible produce all year long. The best way to delve into the bounty is to check out a local farmers' market. Held on Wednesdays, this one is the granddaddy of them all – it's where chefs from the city's most prominent restaurants shop.

17 HOLLYWOOD FARMERS' MARKET

Ivar Avenue &
Selma Avenue
Hollywood ⑦
+1 323 463 3171
hollywoodfarmers market.net

The chefs that haven't stocked up at the Santa Monica market will be here as well when it opens at 8 am on Sunday. With more than 160 vendors of fresh food and artisanal goods, there's no better way to do Sunday brunch than sampling from stall to stall.

18 STUDIO CITY FARMERS' MARKET

2052 Ventura Place
Studio City ⑭
+1 818 655 7744
studiocityfarmers market.com

If you have kids, this is the market to check out: there's an entire play zone devoted to them, featuring pony rides, a petting zoo, a climbing wall, and a train. Wear them out for a nap while you spend Sunday morning shopping for organic produce, grass-fed meats, and just-cut flowers.

19 ALTADENA FARMERS' MARKET

600 W Palm Street
Altadena ⑯
*altadenafarmers
market.com*

An alternative to the massive (and massively popular) Santa Monica Farmers' Market, this is a low-key, late-afternoon market that allows you to shop for locally made (and grown) goods in the quaint enclave of Altadena on Wednesdays. As dusk settles over the San Gabriel Mountains, you can picnic in Loma Alta Park.

20 MALIBU FARMERS' MARKET

23555 Civic
Center Way
Malibu ①
*cornucopia
foundation.net*

On Sunday mornings, the parking lot of the Malibu Library transforms into what is the tony beach community's most popular (and democratic) social event. With plenty of prepared foods, including a great selection of vegan and gluten-free items, there's plenty to snack on while you pick from sun-kissed produce.

16 SANTA MONICA DOWNTOWN FARMERS' MARKET

5 *iconic*
LA STREET FOODS

21 **BACON WRAPPED HOT DOGS**
VARIOUS LOCATIONS
AT: DIRT DOG
2528 S Figueroa St
University Park ⑩
+1 213 749 1813
dirtdogla.com

The bacon-wrapped hot dog is one of the most famous of LA street foods. Cooked on portable flat-top grills with onions and peppers, the real deal can often be found on the sidewalks outside clubs and bars downtown. The one at Dirt Dog, however, demands less searching.

22 **FRUIT STANDS**
VARIOUS LOCATIONS
10074 Washington Boulevard
Culver City ④

On sidewalks across the city you will find small carts, topped by colorful umbrellas, like this one run by Jose Rodriquez, that display a rainbow of fruit, waiting to be cut and served. Order specific fruits or *con todos,* which yields an array of fresh melons, cucumber, mango, oranges, jicama, and sometimes coconut, served with lime, salt, and chili in a plastic bag with a fork.

23 ELOTE

751 N Echo Park Ave
(Echo Park Lake)
Echo Park ⑮

A popular Mexican treat and iconic LA street food, *elote* is grilled corn served with condiments such as mayonnaise, crema, chili powder, lime, and some sort of cheese *(queso fresco* or *cotija)*. It can be served on the cob or as this popular elotero prefers, in Styrofoam bowls, from a cart.

24 DOLLAR HITS

2422 Temple Street
Westlake ⑩
+1 213 399 3160

Though there is a truck involved, the fact that most of the offerings from it – mostly skewers of various meats and fish balls – are then cooked (by you, this is a DIY operation) on grills lining the pavement makes this Filipino street-food provider less a food truck and more a sidewalk affair.

25 RASPADOS
AT: BIONICOS LA PALAPA

5560 N Figueroa St
Highland Park ⑮
+1 323 255 2311

A *raspado* is a Mexican shaved-ice drink, served slushy and made with lots of fruit; it can be either sweet or spicy. These colorful, icy drinks are the best way to keep cool on LA's hottest days and can be found served from coolers and carts in parks – the best are in Latino neighborhoods, of course.

5
STRIP-MALL
gems

---

26 JITLADA

5233 W Sunset
Boulevard
Hollywood ⑦
+1 323 667 9809
jitladala.com

This is the Thai restaurant every foodie
talks about, and for good reason: the
food is amazing and offers both familiar
fare and more obscure Southern Thai
specialties. But it's co-owner Sarintip 'Jazz'
Singsanong who keeps me coming back –
she makes everyone from food critics to
celebs to first-timers feel at home.

27 TROIS MEC

716 Highland Avenue
Hollywood ⑦
+1 323 484 8588
troismec.com

All the idiosyncratic hallmarks of
a hip LA restaurant come together here:
first, the odd location (a former pizza
parlor whose signage still remains);
second, a unique reservations and
payment system; and third, the presence
of a world-renowned chef (Ludovic
Lefebvre) cooking his most personal
food for only a handful of patrons.

28 RUEN PAIR

5257 Hollywood
Boulevard
Hollywood ⑦
+1 323 466 0153
ruenpairthaila.com

Another Thai restaurant with an expansive menu (although it leans more Thai-Chinese) located in the part of East Hollywood known as Thai Town; not only is Ruen Pair a sure bet for delicious food, it's also open until 3 am. So enjoy its celebrated turnip omelet and sautéed morning glory.

29 SUSHI GEN

422 E 2nd Street
Downtown/
Little Tokyo ⑲
+1 213 617 0552
sushigen-dtla.com

You will become intimately familiar with the surrounding strip mall as you wait in line for a seat to open up at this popular sushi spot. Crowds come because for more than 30 years Sushi Gen has been providing high-quality traditional sushi at the most affordable prices around. Also, a favorite of off-duty chefs.

30 PAPILLES

6221 Franklin Ave
Hollywood ⑦
+1 323 871 2026
papillesla.com

A casual bistro located near the 101 Freeway on-ramp, this neighborhood gem offers a prix fixe dinner of seasonal, French-inspired fare. Inspired by the bistronomique movement, chef Jordan Rosas creates sophisticated meals offered in a relaxed setting.

5 unique
LA FOOD COURTS

---

31 **FAR EAST PLAZA**
727 N Broadway
Chinatown ⑩

This 1976 structure houses one of the first ethnic food courts built in the US; today, it's under a massive resurgence with good eats in every shop. From the historic (Ten Ren, Fortune) to the hip (Chego, Howlin' Rays, Unit 120), some of the hottest – literally and figuratively – restaurants are here.

32 **GRAND CENTRAL MARKET**
317 S Broadway
Downtown ⑩
+1 213 624 2378
*grandcentral
market.com*

This Los Angeles landmark (located in the historic Homer Laughlin Building since 1917) is an open-air emporium of food and drink stalls. Like the Far East Plaza, it's a bustling mix of the old and new where one thing is certain: you will eat a great meal. Quintessentially LA.

33 **WESTFIELD CENTURY CITY**
10250 Santa Monica
Boulevard
Century City ⑤
+1 310 277 3898
*westfield.com/
centurycity*

There's a Shake Shack here – the infamous burger joint imported from NYC – as well as the soon-to-open outpost for another famous New York institution, Mario Batali's Eataly. If those two don't inspire lines long enough for you, hop in the queue for Din Tai Fung, the Taiwanese restaurant famous for its incredible soup dumplings.

34 KOREATOWN PLAZA

928 S Western Ave
Koreatown ⑨
+1 213 382 1234
koreatownplaza.com

This three-story shopping mall has all manner of retail shops and services but you are here for the food court, located in the lower level. Here locals enjoy quick and inexpensive Korean (or Korean-influenced) food, including dumplings, rice cakes, *soondae* (blood sausage), porridge, and an especially large (share it) *tonkatsu* plate.

35 ORIGINAL FARMERS MARKET

6333 W 3rd Street
Fairfax ⑧
+1 323 933 9211
farmersmarketla.com

Since 1934, folks have been meeting at 'Fairfax and 3rd' for shopping at more than 100 different vendors – produce stands, gourmet food purveyors, and restaurant stalls offering everything from sushi or Korean BBQ to po'boys and tacos, enjoyed outside. This is a dining hall for everyone; if your grandparents visited LA, they came here.

32 GRAND CENTRAL MARKET

5

SECRET MENUS

36 IN-N-OUT BURGER
VARIOUS LOCATIONS
+1 800 786 1000
in-n-out.com

Most Angelenos would argue these are the best fast-food burgers in America. Part of the charm is in ordering – the menu is simple but there are a myriad of ways to customize your burger, most of which are colorfully named ('4×4' and 'animal style') and have been passed around like urban legends. A key is available on the chain's website.

37 BAR AMA
118 W 4th Street
Downtown ⑩
+1 213 687 8002
bar-ama.com

This is the more casual of Josef Centeno's (Bäco Mercat) restaurants, where his 'Nana's Frito Pie' is part of his creative take on Tex-Mex. Not on the menu but much lauded are his 'puffy tacos', tortillas deep-fried so that they puff up into clouds that are filled with your choice of meat.

38 SPAGO
176 N Canon Drive
Beverly Hills ⑤
+1 310 385 0880
wolfgangpuck.com/dining/spago

Wolfgang Puck, the chef who has pretty much defined fine dining in LA and is well known for his innovative Asian-European fusion food, served tuna cones at the original location of Spago on the Sunset Strip. Since then, they have become a favorite of the Oscars that Puck caters.

39 NIGHT + MARKET SONG

3322 W Sunset Blvd
Silver Lake ⑫
+1 323 665 5899
nightmarketsong.com

I'm not sure you'll find another sandwich anywhere that mixes ranch dressing and green papaya marinated in fish sauce and lime, but here it is on the fried chicken sandwich. This off-menu item was first created as a staff snack; now it's become a phenomenon. The brined then fried chicken thigh retains its juiciness and the toppings add a Thai-influenced tang.

40 BELCAMPO RESTAURANT & BUTCHER SHOP

1026 Wilshire Blvd
Santa Monica ②
+1 424 744 8008
belcampo.com

Belcampo raises its own meat on a farm in Northern California, ensuring the best in quality, and while other outposts are more casual burger affairs, this one is swankier – a real restaurant. Plus, it's the only Belcampo that serves the off-menu poutine – Kennebec fries topped with cheese curds, caramelized onions, and a red-wine demi glace.

39 NIGHT + MARKET SONG

5 of the best
BREAKFASTS

---

41 SQIRL

720 N Virgil Ave #4
Silver Lake ⑬
+1 323 284 8147
sqirlla.com

Though she started by selling her jams at local farmers' markets, Jessica Koslow is now the poster child for what food critics are calling the 'new California cooking'. This tiny cafe, which serves only breakfast and lunch, showcases her creativity; everything is worth waiting in the line, especially the sorrel pesto rice bowl.

42 FOUNTAIN COFFEE ROOM

AT: BEVERLY HILLS HOTEL
9641 Sunset Blvd
Beverly Hills ⑤
+1 310 276 2251
dorchester collection.com

Even the wallpaper here is iconic – the original Martinique Banana Leaf wallpaper, created for the Fountain when it was built in 1949. It's rare to find a vintage soda fountain that maintains charm without being self-consciously retro. This is one that does; breakfast here is a lovely trip back in time.

43 MB POST

1142 Manhattan Ave
Manhattan Beach ⑰
+1 310 545 5405
eatmbpost.com

In many ways MB Post is the opposite of Sqirl – a cavernous, loud restaurant, modeled on the public house. But like Sqirl, it has the personal touch of its chef (David LeFevre) in food that showcases LA's bountiful produce and cultural diversity. Plus, eating their bacon cheddar buttermilk biscuits this close to the beach? Heaven.

44 HUCKLEBERRY CAFÉ

1014 Wilshire Blvd
Santa Monica ②
+1 310 451 2311
huckleberrycafe.com

The founders of this casual artisan bakery and cafe fell in love while working at another nearby restaurant, so maybe some of the sweetness of their pastries comes from genuine affection. Though the baked goods are costly, they are worth every cent: well-made croissants (try the prosciutto-stuffed) and biscuits that melt in your mouth.

45 EMPRESS HARBOR SEAFOOD RESTAURANT

111 N Atlantic
Boulevard #350
Monterey Park ⑯
+1 626 300 8833
empressharbor.net

Sometimes only dim sum will do and this is a classic pushcart place. It's the tip of the iceberg as far as exploring the wealth of incredible Chinese food available in the San Gabriel Valley goes, but here the egg tarts are flaky, the taro cakes delicious, and the service impeccable.

5

PERFECT PATIOS

---

46 CLIFF'S EDGE

3626 W Sunset Blvd
Silver Lake ⑬
+1 323 666 6116
cliffsedgecafe.com

With LA's gorgeous weather, it's a crime we aren't eating every meal outside. Who would guess, sitting in the shade of a huge tree on the patio at Cliff's Edge among lush greenery, that you are steps away from the bustling Sunset Junction? A perfect respite after you shop Sunset Boulevard.

47 EVELEIGH

8752 W Sunset Blvd
West Hollywood ⑥
+1 424 239 1630
theeveleigh.com

The frenzy of the nearby Sunset Strip disappears on the garden patio of this 1923 former residence. Situated on what was once an orchard, verdant greenery (actually edibles used for the kitchen) surrounds diners, and just above the garden's boundaries city lights sparkle in the night.

48 MALIBU FARM

23000 Pacific Coast
Highway
Malibu ①
+1 310 456 1112
malibu-farm.com

The view doesn't get better than this – on the pier; you are basically sitting in the ocean. Both the restaurant and the cafe offer outdoor seating and it is certainly worth the wait to get it. The food, much of it coming from the namesake farm, is delicious, but the ocean breeze is the best.

49 REDBIRD

114 E 2nd Street
Downtown ⑩
+1 213 788 1191
redbird.la

Neal Fraser's flagship restaurant, located inside the rectory of the former St. Vibiana's Cathedral, is a great place to sample his take on modern American cuisine. The main dining room is the gorgeous courtyard patio that features a retractable roof. The space, in the middle of downtown, manages to be both awe-inspiring and comfortable.

50 EVERSON ROYCE BAR

1936 E 7th Street
Downtown/
Arts District ⑩
+1 213 335 6166
erbla.com

The simple neon sign reading 'bar' out front gives no idea of the riches inside. This popular neighborhood watering hole has a huge patio out back and a menu of 'snacks' that make a delicious meal. The cheeseburgers are some of the best around and the comfortable setting feels like a beautifully lit backyard.

46 CLIFF'S EDGE

5 *places to*

FEED YOUR SOUL

---

51 CAFE GRATITUDE
639 N Larchmont
Boulevard
Larchmont Village ⑦
+1 323 580 6383
cafegratitude.com

There are five locations of this plant-based restaurant in LA, a vegetarian cafe you can comfortably take carnivores to (there's even a play on In-N-Out's Double Double burger on the menu). It's the kind of hippy-dippy health-food joint LA is known for and while the sentiments are real, they are also done with a wink.

52 INN OF THE SEVENTH RAY
128 Old Topanga
Canyon Road
Topanga
+1 310 455 1311
innoftheseventhray.com

Situated in what feels like a deep, enchanted forest, this is not only one of LA's most beautiful restaurants, it's one of the most vibey. Food is prepared 'charged with the vibration of the violet flame of the Seventh Ray' and might transport you to a higher plane. From my magical times there, I'd say yes.

52 INN OF THE SEVENTH RAY

53 GRACIAS MADRE

8905 Melrose Avenue
West Hollywood ⑥
+1 323 978 2170
graciasmadreweho.com

This Mexican vegan restaurant (cofounded by the folks from Cafe Gratitude) eschews any 'crunchy' aesthetic – the space is airy and chic. Especially interesting is the beverage program with its creative cocktails, including boozed-up snow cones and 'high vibe' drinks made with cold-pressed Cannabidiol oil.

54 BAROO

5706 Santa Monica
Boulevard
Hollywood ⑦
+1 323 929 9288
baroola.strikingly.com

Proclaimed by *Bon Appetit* magazine to be one of the best new restaurants in the US, this tiny, unmarked spot in a busy strip mall is hardly under the radar. But its chef's inspired take on Korean food and his experimentation into fermentation deserve praise. Named for the bowl Buddhist monks eat from, there is a decidedly spiritual bent to the cooking.

55 LITTLE PINE

2870 Rowena Avenue
Silver Lake ⑫
+1 323 741 8148
littlepinerestaurant.com

Owned by the musician Moby, this stylish neighborhood restaurant serves exclusively vegan cuisine. (If you know anything about Moby, you know he's a devout vegan.) Open for weekend brunch and dinner. All proceeds from the Mediterranean-inspired menu go to animal welfare organizations.

5
POWER LUNCH
spots

---

56 **THE POLO LOUNGE**
AT: BEVERLY HILLS HOTEL
9641 Sunset Blvd
Beverly Hills ⑤
+1 310 887 2777
*dorchester
collection.com*

This is a relic of old Hollywood with great lore: Marlene Dietrich was once not permitted in because she was wearing pants (she checked out of the hotel immediately and the restaurant soon changed its policy); one of Sinatra's pals threw an ashtray at a patron who asked the table to quiet down.

57 **DRAGO CENTRO**
525 S Flower Street
Downtown ⑩
+1 213 228 8998
dragocentro.com

This space includes a former bank vault, which maybe tells you all you need to know: this is a place to come when the bill is being paid by a corporate account. Enjoy modern Italian cuisine with a wonderful view of Central Library.

58 **GJELINA**
1429 Abbot Kinney
Boulevard
Venice ③
+1 310 450 1429
gjelina.com

This is the spot for the Silicon Beach crowd – the tech CEOs and bloggers who work nearby frequent this rustic yet elegant restaurant that serves farm-to-table fare. Note: there are no substitutions or changes allowed to items on the menu. Apparently, tech leaders respond to such limitations.

59 THE IVY

113 N Robertson
Boulevard
Beverly Grove ⑤
+1 310 274 8303
theivyrestaurants.com

Known as a place to spot B-list celebrities, who often lunch here while shopping along the nearby boutiques, it seems less a cozy restaurant to me than a backdrop for the paparazzi. Offering homespun food at exorbitant prices, the Ivy is a great place for reality TV stars.

60 NOBU MALIBU

22706 Pacific Coast
Highway
Malibu ①
+1 310 317 9140
noburestaurants.com

This beachfront restaurant offers incredible views of the ocean from almost every table, but the patio with the fresh ocean breeze is especially nice. Nobu Matsuhisa's sushi and other fare blends Japanese technique with California ingredients – and much of what you are eating tastes as if it sprung straight from the sea.

60 NOBU MALIBU

5

ALL-NIGHT EATERIES

61 **THE ORIGINAL PANTRY CAFÉ**
877 S Figueroa Street
Downtown ⑩
+1 213 972 9279
pantrycafe.com

There are no locks on the front door of the Pantry, which has never been closed since opening in 1924 (although it's only been at this location since 1950). Owned by former LA mayor Richard Riordan, this is the spot for late-night diner food with massive portions of pancakes, ham, and eggs to soak up the evening's regrets.

62 **CANTER'S DELI**
419 N Fairfax Avenue
Fairfax ⑧
+1 323 651 2030
cantersdeli.com

This traditional Jewish deli, owned by the fourth generation of the Canter family, is one of California's oldest delis. It's beloved by locals and celebrities, who slip in for late-night noshes. Back in the day, The Doors and Frank Zappa frequented the Kibitz Room, the adjacent cocktail lounge; today it hosts local bands.

63 **HODORI**
1001 S Vermont Avenue #101
Koreatown ⑨
+1 213 383 3554
hodorirestaurants.com

A late-night institution in Koreatown and revelers fill this busy home-style Korean restaurant well into the wee hours of the morning. It's not the best food in Koreatown (if you were looking for the best, you wouldn't be out at 3 am), but it's solid and soaks up a substantial amount of alcohol.

64 TOI ON SUNSET

7505 ½ W Sunset
Boulevard
West Hollywood ⑥
+1 323 874 8062
toirockinthaifood.com

The décor is basically dorm room if you went to college in the late 80s/early 90s and liked punk rock. It's messy, loud, and wonderful here – and the Thai food, a mix of traditional and Americanized, is good too. Only open until 4 am, it was at one time director Quentin Tarantino's favorite place to write.

65 PACIFIC DINING CAR

1310 W 6th Street
Westlake (near
Downtown) ⑩
+1 213 483 6000
pacificdiningcar.com

In the 1920s, when oil speculators besieged LA and Pacific Electric Red Cars crisscrossed the city, an eccentric couple decided to build a replica of a railway dining car as a restaurant. Still family-owned, this timeless steakhouse is open 24/7 and serves breakfast, lunch, afternoon tea, happy hour, dinner, and a late-night menu.

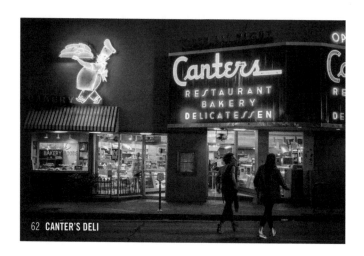

62 CANTER'S DELI

The 5
SWEETEST TREATS
to savor

---

66 FAIR OAKS PHARMACY

1526 Mission Street
South Pasadena ⑯
+1 626 799 1414
fairoakspharmacy.net

Located on a charming street in South Pas, this corner drug store still operates its soda fountain, serving old-fashioned phosphates, lime rickeys, or egg creams. Plus, there are sandwiches for lunch and, of course, ice cream. Once a popular stop along the famous Route 66, the building has been restored to its full glory.

67 FRANKIELUCY BAKESHOP

3116 ½ W Sunset Boulevard
Silver Lake ⑫
+1 323 285 1458
frankielucybakeshop.com

This cute bakery is a collaboration between Crème Caramel L.A. and Found Coffee in Eagle Rock that specializes in Filipino-inspired desserts. Ube, the beautifully hued purple yam, plays a central role in several of the specialties, including the 'not-to-be-missed ube upside down pie' and 'ube latte'.

68 DONUT FRIEND

5107 York Boulevard
Highland Park ⑬
+1 213 995 6191
donutfriend.com

We are all about customizing in LA, even donuts. At this hip spot in Highland Park, you pick your kind of donut, a filling, and toppings. Or you can choose one of their creations, which reveal the staff's sense of humor and love of rock 'n' roll, such as 'Coconut of Conformity' and 'Chocolate from the Crypt'.

69 SCOOPS

712 N Heliotrope Dr
Hollywood ⑦
+1 323 906 2649

This no-frills ice-cream shop has hands-down the most creative flavors in town, and now the indie has expanded to open five shops around LA (there's even one next door to Donut Friend, so double up). That means you can get your brown bread, the shop's most popular flavor, in several different neighborhoods.

70 COOLHAUS

8588 Washington
Boulevard
Culver City ④
+1 310 838 5559
cool.haus

In a clever homage to architecture, this company makes towering ice-cream sandwiches from seasonal and local ingredients. Originally selling their sammies from a single truck, Coolhaus expanded (ten trucks) and has two stores in LA. Choose a premade sammie or build a 'cool haus' of your own by picking a cookie flavor and ice cream.

66. FAIR OAKS PHARMACY

68. DONUT FRIEND

5

CLASSIC LA JOINTS

71 **THE APPLE PAN**
10801 W Pico Blvd
West LA ⑤
+1 310 475 3585

There might be no better diner in all of
LA – the Apple Pan is a beloved institution
on the Westside, and its hickory burger
is not to be missed. Sitting at the U-
shaped counter, talking to strangers and
the long-time staff, you'll feel you slipped
back to the 1940s. And there's pie: fruit
(gotta try the apple, right?) and cream.

72 **COLE'S FRENCH
DIP & PHILIPPE
THE ORIGINAL**
Cole's:
118 E 6th Street
Downtown ⑩
+1 213 622 4090
*213hospitality.com/
project/coles*

Practically within walking distance
are two places that both claim to be the
inventors of the French dip sandwich –
a decades-long dispute between two
landmark restaurants. Cole's, opened
in 1908, is the oldest saloon in the city;
whereas Philippe boasts a 45-cent
cup of coffee to enjoy alongside the
famous sandwich.

Philippe:
1001 Alameda Street
Downtown ⑩
+1 213 628 3781
philippes.com

73 THE TRAILS CAFÉ

2333 Fern Dell Drive
Griffith Park ⑪
+1 323 871 2102

Though it doesn't have enough history to be 'classic', this little stand selling wholesome sandwiches and handmade pastries in the park captures one aspect of what makes LA special: within a few minutes of driving, the most urban of settings can become totally wild. This woodland wonderland coexists perfectly with its home city.

74 THE GALLEY

2442 Main Street
Santa Monica ②
+1 310 452 1934
thegalleyrestaurant.net

Santa Monica's oldest restaurant captures the charming funkiness of the beach city's soul. First, there's the mixed-aged clientele, mostly locals enjoying a casual dinner or a drink at the South Seas Bar. The rattan-heavy décor is a mix of memorabilia from the 1934 film *Mutiny on the Bounty* and World War II propaganda posters.

75 ZANKOU CHICKEN

5065 W Sunset Blvd
Hollywood ⑦
+1 323 665 7842
zankouchicken.com

When a place is name-checked in a Beck song ('Debra'), you know it's important. Opened in 1984 by the Iskenderian family, who brought their garlic sauce and chicken recipe from Beirut, Zankou has since expanded to include other locations. Inexpensive and delicious, this chicken is loved by LA.

FROLIC ROOM

40 PLACES
FOR A DRINK

5
SPEAKEASY-STYLE
bars

———————————

76 **DEL MONTE SPEAKEASY**
52 Windward Avenue
Venice ③
+1 310 392 4040
townhousevenice.com

This is one of the oldest bars in LA and once was a genuine speakeasy accessible from the grocery store that was above (now the Townhouse bar) via a trapdoor. The clandestine setup was used during Prohibition to shuttle illegal liquor from ships docked at the Venice pier to nearby hotels.

77 **THE WALKER INN**
3612 W 6th Street
Koreatown ⑨
+1 213 263 2709
thewalkerinnla.com

Accessed through a button in the back of the Normandie Club, this small, stylish bar is a laboratory for cocktail innovation. But instead of mixology pretense, there's just whimsy and fun – plus an adjacent hotel in case you want to make a night of it.

78 **THE VARNISH**
118 E 6th Street
Downtown ⑩
+1 213 264 7089
*213hospitality.com/
the-varnish*

A storage room in the back of the historic saloon Cole's French Dip was transformed by Eric Alperin and Sasha Petraske into this speakeasy-style bar that focuses on meticulously made cocktails. When it opened in 2009, The Varnish was the epicenter of LA's craft cocktail movement and nearly a decade later it continues to set the standard.

79 **EXHIBITION ROOM**

1117 E Wardlow Road
Long Beach ⑰
+1 562 826 2940
theexhibitionroom.com

Make a reservation and receive a text message with the night's password to enter this Prohibition era-themed neo-speakeasy. Then, enter through a phone booth located in the back of another bar. The result? Time travel and craft cocktails. There's even a collection of cocktail memorabilia from the Long Beach Historical Society.

80 **LA DESCARGA**

1159 N Western Ave
Hollywood ⑦
+1 323 466 1324
ladescargala.com

A Cuban-themed rum and cigar bar that has a dramatic entrance (we don't want to spoil the fun!), but the speakeasy-style entrance is just the beginning. Inside is a live band playing cumbia music (and there are salsa dancing lessons on certain nights). Sometimes there's a show and always, there's the backroom bar, which boasts a selection of more than one hundred handpicked rums.

80 LA DESCARGA

5 traditional
TIKI BARS

---

81 DAMON'S
317 N Brand Blvd
Glendale ⑮
+1 818 507 1510
damonsglendale.com

This Polynesian-themed steakhouse has been family-owned for nearly 76 years, half of which have been in its current location. So the vibe here isn't retro – it's real. This is a classic neighborhood steakhouse, albeit with a serious tiki theme and the requisite tropical drinks and cuisine. Happy hour is a deal.

82 LUAU LARRY'S
509 Crescent Avenue
Catalina Island
+1 310 510 1919
luaularrys.com

A great day trip is to take the ferry to nearby Catalina Island; ports in San Pedro, Long Beach, Newport Beach, and Dana Point will get you there. This tiki-themed oyster bar (and institution) in Avalon will make you feel as if you've traveled far – though you'll spy the city's lights in the distance.

83 TONGA HUT
12808 Victory Blvd
North Hollywood ⑭
+1 818 769 0708
tongahut.com

Once again, there's no faux retro vibe here: this is an original tiki bar, opened in 1958, when the tiki craze was at its height. Today, they are still dolling out neon-hued tropical drinks that pack a serious punch and the décor retains its mid-century glory.

84 **THE PACIFIC SEAS**
AT: CLIFTON'S REPUBLIC
648 S Broadway
Downtown ⑩
+1 213 627 1673
cliftonsla.com/
pacific-seas

One of many bars in the wonderland that is Clifton's, this homage to tiki is also a tribute to the cafeteria chain's history, featuring artifacts from an original Pacific Seas and other legendary departed tiki bars. The fantastic visual feast pairs perfectly with the Singapore Slings and Mai Tais.

85 **TIKI-TI**
4427 Sunset Blvd
Hollywood ⑦
+1 323 699 9381
tiki-ti.com

One of the most beloved bars in town also happens to be the smallest – there are only twelve stools and a handful of tables. But at this bar, family-owned and -operated since 1961, the recipes for several of the most famous drinks – Zombie, Navy Grog – descended directly from the original Don the Beachcomber.

85 TIKI-TI

The 5 most lively
PLACES TO DANCE

---

86 THE AIRLINER
2419 N Broadway
Lincoln Heights ⑮
+1 323 221 0771

This two-story club has two bars and a big dance floor and is divey and inviting to all. There's dancing several nights a week with DJs who play a range of hip hop, indie rock, and electronic music. Plus, some live acts and a kitchen that serves bacon-wrapped hotdogs.

87 THE AVALON
1735 Vine Street
Hollywood ⑦
+1 323 462 8900
avalonhollywood.com

This 1926 theater building is a historic landmark that once hosted The Beatles' first West Coast performance and throughout the 1960s was the site of television's 'The Hollywood Palace Variety Show'. Today it's a bumping place for electronic music, with all the DJ superstars stopping in for sets.

88 LA CITA
336 S Hill Street
Downtown ⑩
+1 213 687 7111
lacitabar.com

Once a historic Mexican dance hall, there's still lots of good dancing to be had at this hacienda-style building. The clientele – as diverse as the city itself – packs the festive dance floor for alternative Latin, as well as rockabilly, punk, and hip-hop music from live bands and or DJs.

89 THE ECHOPLEX

1822 W Sunset Blvd
Echo Park ⑫
+1 213 413 8200
theecho.com

One of the coolest small venues for live music in LA, this is where in 2013 the Rolling Stones performed a secret show for fans. It's a great, no-pretense place to see some of the best emerging bands and has regular dance nights including Dub Club, on Wednesdays, a highly regarded reggae night.

90 PRECINCT DTLA

357 S Broadway
Downtown ⑩
+1 213 628 3112
precinctdtla.com

The name comes from the fact that the location of this club was formerly an office for the Department of Corrections; today it's downtown's biggest gay club. There's a fantastic semi-enclosed patio that stretches around the place and dance nights, drag nights, and just good fun nights.

88 LA CITA

5 fun
BARCADES

---

91 BLIPSY BARCADE
369 N Western Ave
Koreatown ⑨
+1 323 461 7067

A barcade is where you can drink and play video games, preferably vintage arcade games. Blipsy's, marked only by a Pac-Man ghost outside the door, is the quintessential example – a divey bar with occasional DJs crammed full of old arcade consoles and pinball games. It's cash only, so bring a fistful of quarters.

92 BUTTON MASH
1391 W Sunset Blvd
Echo Park ⑬
+1 213 250 9903

This is a Chuck E. Cheese's for grown-ups: a hip bar and restaurant that serves fantastic Asian-fusion food and is chock full of golden-era arcade games. There's great beer and wine selections, dozens of 1980s video games, chicken wings, and spam fried rice. What could be better?

93 EIGHTYTWO
707 E 4th Place
Downtown/
Arts District ⑩
+1 213 626 8200
eightytwo.la

This full bar offers craft cocktails and a large selection of beer and wine (as well as non-alcoholic selections) alongside a rotating collection of 50 classic arcade and pinball machines. There's a nice, big patio and often on weekends a line to get in since the place reaches capacity.

94 **PINS AND NEEDLES**
   1623 Allesandro St
   Echo Park ⑫
   +1 323 313 9449
   pinsandneedlesla.com

This is a barcade minus the bar; instead, it's heaven for pinball fans – a huge band practice space that has restored vintage pinball machines in the lobby. The hours range and there's no food or drink, so go to play pinball only and call first.

95 **THE ONE UP**
   13625 Ventura Blvd
   Sherman Oaks ⑭
   +1 818 849 5181
   theoneup.com

This hip cocktail lounge has American-style bar snacks (sliders, tacos, hot dogs) and drinks along with eight or so consoles that offer a selection of classic video games. Play is free (no quarters necessary) and the vibe is Valleyites on date night.

92 BUTTON MASH

5

HOLLYWOOD WATERING HOLES

---

96 BAR MARMONT

8171 W Sunset
Boulevard
West Hollywood ⑥
+1 323 650 0575
chateaumarmont.com

It doesn't get more Hollywood than the legendary Chateau Marmont hotel, which is next door to this, the hotel's adjacent cocktail lounge and restaurant. You are close enough to feel the ghosts next door while enjoying classic cocktails in a cozy and sexy atmosphere.

97 BOARDNER'S

1652 N Cherokee Ave
Hollywood ⑦
+1 323 462 9621
boardners.com

Operating off the famed boulevard for more than 75 years, this no-frills neighborhood bar has drawn a solid cast of characters over the years, including Errol Flynn, W.C. Fields, and Ed Wood. Also, Elizabeth Short, the aspiring actress whose unsolved death became known as the Black Dahlia murder, was a regular.

98 FROLIC ROOM

6245 Hollywood Blvd
Hollywood ⑦
+1 323 462 5890

This is a dive bar with great history located in the heart of Hollywood. Legend is this bar was originally a speakeasy that served players from the Pantages Theatre next door named for its proprietor, Freddy Frolic. Don't miss the fabulous neon sign or the Al Hirschfeld mural.

99 HARLOWE

7321 Santa Monica
Boulevard
West Hollywood ⑥
+1 323 876 5839
harlowebar.com

While there's nothing historic about this bar, its atmosphere summons up Hollywood's golden era with its Art Deco décor and the quality of service. There's a full food menu and cocktails on tap; go early for the specials and the relaxed atmosphere. It gets busy after 9 pm.

100 MUSSO & FRANK GRILL

6667 Hollywood Blvd
Hollywood ⑦
+1 323 467 7788
mussoandfrank.com

A martini at this venerable Hollywood institution is a must. Not only is it the best in town, it's a true taste of classic LA. Since 1919, these leather booths have seen it all: film's biggest players ate and drank here (Charlie Chaplin, Bogart & Bacall, Elizabeth Taylor), and many of the 20th century's best American writers (Fitzgerald, Faulkner, Chandler) met in the backroom.

98 FROLIC ROOM

100 MUSSO & FRANK GRILL

The 5 best
ROOFTOP BARS

---

101 E.P. & L.P.
603 N La Cienega
Boulevard
West Hollywood ⑥
+1 310 855 9955
eplosangeles.com

This 'Asian eating house' has cuisine inspired by Vietnam, Fiji and China, and the rooftop bar (the L.P. of the equation) serves casual street-style food and craft cocktails. The sweeping view of the Hollywood Hills and the twinkling basin below is breathtaking. There's also a private bar called Frankie's attached.

102 MAMA SHELTER
6500 Selma Avenue
Hollywood ⑦
+1 323 785 6666
mamashelter.com

This fun hotel and restaurant from the French chain is cheeky and casual, with a colorful, rec-room vibe. The rooftop offers a near 360-degree view of the LA basin, from the Hollywood Sign to the sea. There isn't another view like this at this price point, which is why it's full of twentysomethings.

103 ONYX ROOFTOP LOUNGE

1301 Ocean Avenue
Santa Monica ②
+1 310 394 2791
shangrila-hotel.com

You are not here for the overpriced cocktails, the food, or the décor – you are here to enjoy the incredible view of the ocean, Santa Monica pier, and cliffs of Malibu in the distance. This is a gorgeous place to be at sunset, period.

104 PERCH LA

448 S Hill Street
Downtown ⑩
+1 213 802 1770
perchla.com

This French-inspired bistro has a patio and, up a few more stairs, a rooftop bar that boasts unobstructed views of downtown. Come for happy hour and/or stay for supper; the panoramic views aren't going anywhere.

105 STANDARD HOTEL

550 S Flower Street
Downtown ⑩
+1 213 892 8080
standardhotels.com

Think panoramic views with a party – there's a pool, a dance floor, a beer garden, and waterbed 'pods' at this rooftop bar. But admission is not guaranteed, even for hotel guests. If the scene is too much, here's a tip: the city's big parking decks (The Arclight, the Grove) offer some of the best views, sans the bars.

5 places to summon
LA NOIR

---

106 THE EDISON
108 W 2nd St #101
Downtown ⑩
+1 213 613 0000
edisondowntown.com

Located in a cavernous, subterranean space that once served as LA's first private power plant, this suave cocktail lounge is equal parts steampunk basement (relics like a brick furnace and steam broiler remain) and industrial cathedral. There's often cabaret-style entertainment featuring jazz and blues musicians or aerialists and burlesque dancers.

107 GALLERY BAR
AT: THE BILTMORE HOTEL
506 S Grand Avenue
Downtown ⑩
+1 213 624 1011
millenniumhotels.com

This grand bar has a lot of Prohibition-era history and an adjacent cognac room, but stories about it usually focus on something darker: the Biltmore (not Boardner's) was the last place actress Elizabeth Short, aka the Black Dahlia, was seen alive before her 1947 murder.

108 KING EDDY SALOON
131 E 5th Street
Downtown ⑩
+1 213 629 2023
kingeddysaloon.com

This historic dive bar was recently cleaned up but it's still located in the city's Skid Row. Allegedly a haunt of writers such as Charles Bukowski and John Fante, the bar used to open at 6 am to service a tough crowd (there were buzzers on the steel bathroom doors, operated by the bartenders).

109 THE PRINCE

3198 W 7th Street
Koreatown ⑨
+1 213 389 1586
theprincela.com

There's nothing dark about this bar other
than its moody lighting, which is perfectly
in synch with its classic atmosphere.
No wonder so many films and TV shows
use it as a location *(Chinatown, Mad Men,
New Girl)*. The restaurant is famous for
the Korean fried chicken, but the bar
is famous for looking good.

110 TRAXX/ UNION STATION

800 N Alameda
Street #122
Downtown ⑩
+1 213 625 1999
unionstationla.com

Is there a more glamorous building in LA
than the gorgeous Art Deco Union Station?
It's got the romance of train travel,
enclosed patio gardens, and the grand
waiting room. A cocktail at the station's
fine dining restaurant, Traxx, is just the
thing to catapult you back into the past.

109 THE PRINCE

5 bars for
MORE THAN DRINKS

---

111 THE DRESDEN ROOM
1760 N Vermont Ave
Los Feliz ⑦
+1 323 665 4294
thedresden.com

There are two reasons this 1954 cocktail lounge continues to inspire: Marty and Elayne, the veteran lounge singers who, five nights a week, croon out standards for an adoring crowd of hipsters, old folk, visitors, and regulars. Also, one of the bars featured in the 1996 film *Swingers*.

112 GOOD TIMES AT DAVEY WAYNE'S
1611 N El Centro Ave
Hollywood ⑦
+1 323 962 3804
goodtimesat daveywaynes.com

This 1970s-themed bar by Mark and Jonnie Houston (who made many of LA's most creative bars) is a fun homage to their late father. The entrance is a tableau of a garage sale where an old refrigerator transports you inside. Along with the abundant shag carpeting, there's a patio with an Airstream trailer that serves spiked snow cones.

113 HIGHLAND PARK BOWL

5621 N Figueroa St
Highland Park ⑮
+1 323 257 2695
highlandparkbowl.com

Dating back to the 1920s, this is the city's oldest bowling alley, which has been restored to its former glory. The vintage décor is full of repurposed items found during the restoration, including old pin machines turned into chandeliers. Other treasures include inventive cocktails (one references *The Big Lebowski*) and Neapolitan-style pizza.

114 JUMBO'S CLOWN ROOM

5153 Hollywood Blvd
Hollywood ⑦
+1 323 666 1187
jumbos.com

This is a pole-dancing club with pedigree – first, it's been family-owned and -operated since opening in 1970, and it's also female-operated. Plus, it's got a serious rock 'n' roll vibe (dancers are often pierced or tattooed, pick their own music, and don't court the crowd), which is why Courtney Love once worked here.

115 THE SPARE ROOM

7000 Hollywood Blvd
Hollywood ⑦
+1 323 769 7296
*spareroom
hollywood.com*

Located in the historic Roosevelt Hotel, this Art Deco-style 'gaming parlor' is full of vintage games, including two beautiful bowling lanes. The cocktail menu is in keeping with the Prohibition-era look, with communal punch bowls and signature drinks like the 'Lucky Smoke'.

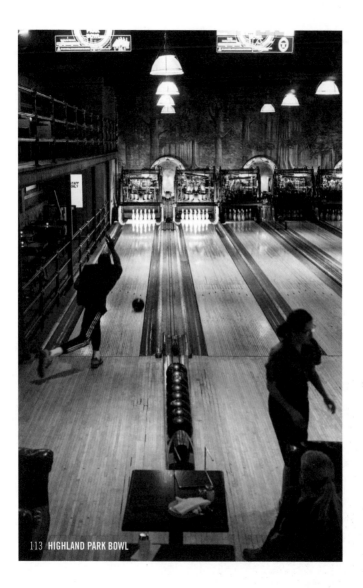

113 HIGHLAND PARK BOWL

ALCHEMY WORKS

65 PLACES TO SHOP

5
FLEA MARKETS
for the best finds

116 ARTISTS & FLEAS LA

740 E 3rd Street
Downtown/
Arts District ⑩
+1 310 900 9987

The Brooklyn-born craft and flea market has come to LA. On Saturdays from 11 am until 5 pm, this parking deck transforms into an outdoor market with vintage goods, locally made crafts and art, and snacks of all sorts. Plus, there are food trucks.

117 MELROSE TRADING POST

7850 Melrose Avenue
Fairfax ⑧
+1 323 655 7679
melrosetradingpost.org

Held on Sundays in the parking lot of Fairfax High School, this flea market is hip, friendly, and full of lovely women in caftans and cowboy boots looking for bargains. The market is a mix of vintage (mostly fashion), antique furniture, and hand-made artisan goods. The treasure hunting includes live music from local musicians.

118 LONG BEACH ANTIQUE FLEA MARKET

4901 E Conant Street
Long Beach ⑰
+1 323 655 5703
*longbeach
antiquemarket.com*

I furnished my first LA apartment from this flea market, scheduled on the third Sunday of every month at the Long Beach Veterans Stadium. More than 800 vendors feature a selection of vintage goods, antique furniture, and collectables. There are 20 acres to cover, so go early and wear sneakers.

119 ROSE BOWL FLEA MARKET

1001 Rose Bowl Drive
Pasadena ⑬
+1 323 560 7469
*rgcshows.com/
rosebowl.aspx*

The granddaddy of them all – for 45 years, this massive flea market with more than 2500 vendors has been held on the second Sunday of the month. Because it is the marathon of markets, wear comfy shoes and bring water. Also, you may spot a few celebrities in the crowd (Diane Keaton is a fan).

120 PCC FLEA MARKET

1570 E Colorado Blvd
Pasadena ⑬
+1 626 585 7906
*pasadena.edu/
community/flea-market*

A low-key alternative to the Rose Bowl, this flea market, held on the first Sunday of the month at Pasadena City College, is manageable and easy. There's even shade over some of the parking deck where vendors sell their vintage and antique treasures.

5 locally loved
BOOKSTORES

121 BOOK SOUP

8818 Sunset Blvd
West Hollywood ⑥
+1 310 659 3110
booksoup.com

This independent bookstore has been located on the Sunset Strip since 1975, which just goes to show that rock 'n' rollers also read. A gem of a store, they often host high-profile and celebrity authors for readings.

122 THE LAST BOOKSTORE

453 S Spring St – G/F
Downtown ⑩
+1 213 488 0599
lastbookstorela.com

This is a bookstore to get lost in, which is easy in this cavernous 22.000-square-foot space. Sure, the name is ironic, but the love for printed matter is real; this is California's largest used and new bookstore, and wandering its floors is entering another world. Don't miss the Arts & Rare Books Annex.

123 LARRY EDMUNDS BOOKSHOP

6644 Hollywood Blvd
Hollywood ⑦
+1 323 463 3273
larryedmunds.com

This is what you wish all the shops were along the famous boulevard. In business for more than 70 years, this store is staffed by people who know and love the movies – they can talk shop for hours and you'll learn lots if you listen. Along with books, there's an incredible collection of film stills and posters.

124 SKYLIGHT BOOKS

1818 N Vermont Ave
Los Feliz ⑦
+1 323 660 1175
skylightbooks.com

The quintessential neighborhood bookstore, this independent seller has been a cornerstone of the community for 20 years. The light-filled space with a tree growing in the middle has a collection of books as eclectic as the clientele, which includes many artists, filmmakers, musicians, and – of course – writers.

125 VROMAN'S BOOKSTORE

695 E Colorado Blvd
Pasadena ⑬
+1 626 449 5320
vromans
bookstore.com

A Pasadena institution, this is California's oldest independent bookstore. Founded in 1894 by Adam Clark Vroman, the shop has a long history; during World War II, Vroman's employees donated and delivered books to interned Japanese Americans at Manzanar.

5 great
RECORD STORES

126 AMOEBA MUSIC

6400 Sunset Blvd
Hollywood ⑦
+1 323 245 6400
amoeba.com

Occupying an entire city block, this is the world's largest independent music store, with an enormous and diverse collection of music and movies. It's great for searching through the record bins, hoping to find a rare pressing or import. The stock changes constantly, and there are frequent in-store performances.

127 ATOMIC RECORDS

3812 W Magnolia
Boulevard
Burbank ⑭
+1 818 848 7090
atomicrecordsla.com

For more than 20 years, Atomic has been open seven days a week buying and selling used vinyl records, CDs, DVDs, and tapes. This welcoming store with a laidback vibe specializes in classic jazz, 1960s rock, punk, new wave, soul, blues, soundtracks, and exotica.

128 PERMANENT RECORDS LA

5116 York Boulevard
Highland Park ⑮
+1 323 739 6141
permanent
recordsla.com

The second shop of the Chicago-based store, the inventory here is mostly vinyl, either out of print or limited releases and new releases and reissues, many of which are from micro-labels. There are also some used CDs and limited-release cassette tapes. There are no music snobs here, just friendly Midwesterners.

129 POO-BAH RECORD SHOP

2636 E Colorado Blvd
Pasadena ⑬
+1 626 449 3359
poobah.com

Open since 1971, this independent record shop has its own imprint that releases limited-edition vinyl and cassettes. There are also plenty of gems to be found in the bins – the shop specializes in underground hip-hop and experimental music, but they've got some of everything.

130 VACATION VINYL

3815 W Sunset Blvd
Silver Lake ⑫
+1 323 666 2111
thejvdasgoat.com

Located in the heart of the Sunset Junction area, this busy and well-curated record store has a great selection of new, independent releases and vintage finds. Also, there are in-store signings and live sessions of local and visiting bands.

130 VACATION VINYL

The 5 best
OUTDOOR MALLS

131 AMERICANA

889 Americana Way
Glendale ⑮
+1 818 637 8982
americanaatbrand.com

This shopping, dining, entertainment, and residential complex was created by developer Rick Caruso (who also did the Grove) to be a modern town square. Along with shops and restaurants, there's a lawn for play and summertime movie screenings, a choreographed fountain, and a trolley that circles all around it.

132 THE GROVE

189 The Grove Drive
Fairfax ⑧
+1 323 900 8080
thegrovela.com

This is the outdoor entertainment complex, connected to the historic Original Farmers Market, that is now the model for successful shopping destinations. With luxury and chain retails, restaurants, and ample entertainment for all ages, there's something for everyone here.

133 THIRD STREET PROMENADE

1351 Third Street
Promenade #201
Santa Monica ②
+1 310 393 8355
downtownsm.com

Located in downtown Santa Monica, this entertainment and retail area spans three blocks of Third Street that are closed to traffic and anchored by Santa Monica Place. There are restaurants, chain and independent shops, and many street performers and buskers.

134 MALIBU COUNTRY MART

3835 Cross Creek Rd
Malibu ①
+1 310 456 7300
*malibucountry
mart.com*

This upscale, outdoor shopping center is close to the beach and full of tony boutiques, cafes, and restaurants. There's a playground for kids and a garden atmosphere. It's so beautiful that even those who hate to shop might not mind a few hours here.

135 BRENTWOOD COUNTRY MART

225 26th Street
Santa Monica ②
+1 310 451 9877
*brentwoodcountry
mart.com*

Intended as the Westside's equivalent of the famed Farmers' Market at Fairfax and Third, this charming red-board structure has shops and stalls arranged around a central courtyard. Since 1948, it's been a staple of the community, as well as a place for the famous to shop.

5 streets for
INDIE BOUTIQUES

---

136 ABBOT KINNEY BOULEVARD

Venice ③
abbotkinneyblvd.com

From jewelry designer Alexis Bittar to shirt maker Steven Alan, this bustling boulevard near the beach offers shops for everyone – women (Heist), men (Shinola Detroit), kids (Salt & Straw). Perhaps the hippest haven on the Westside, there's a fun food-truck event on the first Friday of each month.

137 MONTANA AVENUE

Santa Monica ②
montanaave.com

The shops along this charming tree-lined street are a bit less arty than those on Abbot Kinney but also cater to the affluent, sun-drenched lifestyle. There are great clothing boutiques, shoe stores, and a darling children's bookshop called Every Picture Tells a Story.

138 VENTURA BOULEVARD

Studio City ⑭
ourventurablvd.com

If you're like me, it's impossible not to sing Tom Petty songs (especially 'Free Fallin', which namedrops it) while shopping on this strip in the San Fernando Valley. It's 18 miles long, you're going to need to focus; the blocks between Coldwater Canyon and Laurel Canyon Boulevards offer the highest yield.

139 **WEST 3RD STREET**
Fairfax ⑧
west3rdstreet.com

The stretch of this street between La Cienega Boulevard and Fairfax Avenue is a wonderful, walkable dining and shopping district. Stores include local designers (Nathalie Seaver), menswear (Douglas Fir), and concept (Liberty Fairs Concept 8366 ½). Unique offerings are Scandinavian candy shop Sockerbit, plastics retailer Plastica, and the travel-themed Flight 001.

140 **YORK BOULEVARD**
Highland Park ⑮

Though gentrification has been ripping through the area, the stores along York are still a mix of the old (Mexican markets, hardware stores) and the new (home décor stores, vintage furniture shops), which gives some specificity to the neighborhood. Anchored at Avenue 50 by the Café de Leche coffee shop and York Park.

136 **ABBOT KINNEY BLVD**

5 *places to*
BUY AN OSCAR DRESS

---

141 BARNEYS NEW YORK

9570 Wilshire Blvd
Beverly Hills ⑤
+1 310 276 4400
barneys.com

You can certainly find a gown at the LA outpost of the famed NYC specialty shop; there are many to choose from and a personal shopping service dedicated to finding the dress. But if it doesn't work out and money is no object, you can just walk down nearby Rodeo Drive.

142 DECADES

8214 Melrose Avenue
West Hollywood ⑥
+1 323 655 1960
decadesinc.com

Personally, if an Academy Award invite came my way, I would head straight to the vintage-gown salon at this celebrated consignment shop. On Melrose for more than two decades, this is one of the best designer resale boutiques, not just in LA but in the world.

143 MAXFIELD

8825 Melrose Avenue
West Hollywood ⑥
+1 310 274 8800
maxfieldla.com

The famed luxury boutique has several shops in LA, but this concrete block one is the best. There are curated high-end designer and vintage collections for men and women, plus books, furniture, and gadgets.

144 THE PAPER BAG PRINCESS

8050 Melrose Avenue
West Hollywood ⑥
+1 310 385 9036
*thepaperbag
princess.com*

This luxury consignment boutique specializes in designer vintage evening and cocktail fashions, so it's chock-full of sexy and glamorous gowns. There are also more casual clothes plus shoes, bags, and a bridal salon.

145 RESURRECTION

8006 Melrose Avenue
West Hollywood ⑥
+1 323 651 5516
resurrectionvintage.com

Another high-end vintage apparel and accessories boutique on Melrose, Resurrection is one of the world's best shops for collectible and historic clothing. There are both glamorous (Chanel, Dior) and avant-garde designers (Watanabe, Westwood) here.

142 DECADES

The 5 best
VINTAGE SHOPS

146 AVALON VINTAGE
106 N Avenue #56
Highland Park ⑮
+1 323 309 7717

This shop, owned by Carmen Hawk, offers an incredible collection of vintage clothes and vinyl, plus the prices are affordable and the staff friendly. Hawk, a former model, was also the one-time design partner of Milla Jovovich – if you remember the Jovovich-Hawk line, Hawk's love of vintage fashion largely inspired it.

147 GOTTA HAVE IT
1516 Pacific Avenue
Venice ③
+1 310 392 5949
gottahaveitvenice.com

Located in the heart of Venice, this consignment shop has some modern brands (high-end only), but the stock and trade is mostly vintage – and it's fabulous! The beach isn't the only place for finding treasure.

148 SHAREEN VINTAGE

1721 N Spring Street
Lincoln Heights ⑩
+1 323 276 6226
shareen.com

Take note: because this vintage emporium does not have dressing rooms, it's a 'girls only' space, and men are not allowed. Founder Shareen Mitchell, if she's there, will hand-style you in vintage glory; she also designs her own collections and was the subject of the reality series *Dresscue Me.*

149 SQUARESVILLE

1800 N Vermont Ave
Los Feliz ⑦
+323 669 8464
squaresvillevintage.com

This two-story neighborhood vintage store is the perfect size – it's well curated in a casual way and easy to peruse before dinner or a movie up the street. You won't feel exhausted from sorting, and you will find fashions a bit edgier here.

150 THE WAY WE WORE

334 S La Brea Avenue
Fairfax ⑧
+1 323 937 0878
thewaywewore.com

This is the closet of the grandma you wish you had – you know, the one who was a silent-era screen star and also danced at Studio 54. Owner Doris Raymond possesses an encyclopedic knowledge of fashion, and every era is represented here. A vintage store so good, they made it a TV show *(LA Frock Stars).*

5 nice places to buy
ACCESSORIES

---

151 CLARE V.

3339 W Sunset Blvd
Silver Lake ⑫
+1 323 665 2476
clarev.com

The designer's flagship store, this boutique is a compendium of classic-looking handbags with modern details, beautiful leather, and significant charm. Clare Vivier makes her line exclusively in Los Angeles, so though the bag looks worldly, it's entirely local.

152 DREAM COLLECTIVE

1404 Micheltorena St
Silver Lake ⑫
+1 323 660 2000
dreamcollective.com

Conveniently located next door to Clare V., this is another designer with a uniquely LA element to her work. This concept store is centered on designer Kathryn Bentley's two lines of jewelry collections – the first is stunningly gorgeous fine jewelry, the second a more affordable, whimsical spinoff that is the namesake of the store.

153 GOORIN BROS. HAT SHOP

141 ½ N Larchmont
Boulevard
Larchmont Village ⑦
+1 323 463 2006
goorin.com

You will need a hat to shade you from the sun while you are in LA, so why not get a stylish one here (or at another location of Goorin Bros. in the city; there are several)? Fedora, porkpie, Panama? All styles are here, with selections for men and for women.

154 L.A. EYEWORKS

7407 Melrose Avenue
West Hollywood ⑥
+1 323 653 8255
laeyeworks.com

For three decades, the duo of designers who founded L.A. Eyeworks, Barbara McReynolds and Gai Gherardi, have expanded the optical imagination. The eyeglasses they make are, like the city itself, anything but boring! Find your funky frames here and see the world in rose-colored lenses.

155 THE MAGNOLIA PARK

3500 W Magnolia
Boulevard
Burbank ⑭
themagpark.com

Named after the neighborhood, this massive shoe and streetwear store is the place to get your kicks, literally. If the sneakers you want are exclusive and rare, and you don't mind that someone else has already worn them (it's designer resale mixed with new), this store has almost every exclusive sneaker you can think of (Yeezy, Jordans).

151 CLARE V.

5 shops for
LA STYLE

156 FRED SEGAL

8100 Melrose Avenue
West Hollywood ⑥
+1 323 651 4129
fredsegal.com

This legendary store set the bar for California chic, the laidback luxe that continues to defy trends and inspire new ones. And it's no wonder: Fred Segal has always been ahead of its time. The store's namesake opened the first 'denim bar', back in 1960. Since then Fred Segal has been the place to see and be seen.

157 LOST & FOUND

6320 Yucca Street
Hollywood ⑦
+1 323 856 5872
lostandfoundshop.com

This collection of shops along Yucca has long been a favorite among low-key fashionistas (it was Goop before Goop). The visionary behind it, owner Jamie Rosenthal, started her boutiques back when it was sketchy to hang out in this part of Hollywood. Now, it's a top shopping spot for many of the city's most stylish.

158 AMERICAN RAG CIE

150 S La Brea Avenue
Fairfax/La Brea ⑧
+1 323 935 3154
americanrag.com

From its founding more than 30 years ago, this popular shop is a mainstay of California culture and, like Fred Segal, captures the high/low fashion mix that LA does like nowhere else. With men and women's clothing, new and vintage, a well-curated selection of shoes and accessories, a 'denim bar', and a restaurant next door with excellent home goods, this is going to take a while.

159 ALCHEMY WORKS

826 E 3rd Street
Downtown/
Arts District ⑩
+1 323 487 1497
alchemyworks.us

Owned by a husband-and-wife team, this concept store is a gallery, a retail shop, and an event space. The goods (handmade watches, longboards, silk dresses) have a sun-kissed LA vibe. You can almost feel the salt water in your hair as you dream about taking home the Fiat Abarth 750 Spyder that sits in the middle of the shop.

160 OOGA BOOGA

943 N Broadway #203
Chinatown
+1 213 617 1105
oogaboogastore.com

Hidden on the second floor of an office building, this tiny shop specializes in independent art, books, zines, music, and clothing. Selected by shop owner Wendy Yao, the objects in this concept shop are from local designers and makers; you're sure to find something at any price point you won't find elsewhere.

5 made-in-LA
CLOTHING DESIGNERS

161 **CAROL YOUNG UNDESIGNED**

1953 ½ Hillhurst Ave
Los Feliz ⑦
+1 323 663 0088
carolyoung.com

This bright shop on a busy strip in Los Feliz offers chic women's clothes and accessories, designed by native Angeleno Carol Young. A former architectural student, Young's line of modern and comfortable clothes utilize eco-friendly fabrics and appeal to the creative urban nomad.

162 **HEDLEY & BENNETT**

3864 S Santa Fe Ave
Vernon ⑰
+1 213 744 1355
hedleyandbennett.com

Based in South Los Angeles, this company makes handmade aprons and market bags using top-grade American canvas, raw Japanese selvage denim, and European linens. These aprons and bags are made to last and worn by most of the high-end wait staffs and kitchen crews in town.

161 CAROL YOUNG UNDESIGNED

163 HEIDI MERRICK

115 W 9th Street
Downtown ⑩
+1 310 424 5520
heidimerrick.com

The daughter of legendary surfboard shaper Al Merrick, this LA designer makes women's clothes and home goods inspired by the Pacific Ocean and the California coast. Her studio is located in the same building as her boutique on a fashion-heavy block downtown, so make sure you wander.

164 MATRUSHKA CONSTRUCTION

3822 W Sunset Blvd
Silver Lake ⑫
+1 323 665 4513
matrushka.com

Founded by two friends who make most of the clothes themselves, this friendly shop offers funky and fun clothes, the likes of which you certainly won't find at the mall. The comfortable dresses and silk-screened t-shirts are hand-sewn. There's also a small selection for men – a seismograph shirt is a perfect LA gift.

165 VENLEY

240 West 37th Place
Downtown ⑩
+1 323 521 1397
wearvenley.com

This athleisure company makes all their clothes here in LA, employing 600 people at their 16-block complex. Their casual workout gear for men and women is what you need to hike Griffith Park, roller-blade around Venice, or sample a yoga class in Santa Monica.

The 5 most stylish
DESIGN
stores

---

166 JUST ONE EYE

7000 Romaine Street
Hollywood ⑦
+1 323 969 9129
justoneeye.com

Howard Hughes once owned this Art Deco building, and his films *Hell's Angels, Scarface,* and *The Outlaw* were edited here. Today it houses a concept shop that gathers together high fashion (Gucci, Lanvin), art pieces, books, and collaborative projects – one of which was a disaster survival kit that contained night-vision goggles and a cashmere blanket.

167 KELLY WEARSTLER

8440 Melrose Avenue
West Hollywood ⑥
+1 323 895 7880
kellywearstler.com

This flagship store from the celebrated interior designer features a selection of luxury goods, furniture, curiosities, vintage books, and bespoke designs hand-picked by Wearstler. Find a one-of-a-kind wonder or an affordable gift – the key chains and collaborative chocolates are fun and chic.

168 MOCA STORE

250 S Grand Avenue
Downtown ⑩
+1 213 621 1710
mocastore.org

The fantastic gift shop that accompanies The Museum of Contemporary Art has artists' books galore plus exhibition catalogues, and the like, but there are also artist editions of prints (Andy Warhol Flavor Paper on sale!) and something for every price point. Need a Devo Energy Dome? They're here.

169 MODERNICA

7366 Beverly Blvd
Fairfax ⑧
+1 323 933 0383
modernica.net

Lovers of mid-century modern design classics will feel right at home in this showroom. For 25 years, this locally owned and operated company has been crafting Case Study furniture. In fact, they use the same machinery used to fabricate the original Eames chairs for their rainbow-hued fiberglass shell chairs.

170 OK

1716 Silverlake Blvd
Silver Lake ⑫
+1 323 666 1868
okthestore.com

The modern homewares and gifts at this small boutique are both functional and beautiful – objects that would easily be at home in some of the nearby Neutra homes. There are Comme des Garçons wallets, a gorgeous selection of local jewelers, and whimsical kids toys.

The 5 most famous
TATTOO PARLORS

---

171 ALCHEMY TATTOO

2854 W Sunset Blvd
Silver Lake ⑫
+1 323 666 1313
alchemytattoola.com

Open seven days a week, this custom tattoo studio specializes in American traditional tattoos (their well-written blog even explains the history and meaning of many traditional tattoos). If you want an old-school panther or any kind of traditional sailor tattoo, this is the place to go.

172 AMERICAN ELECTRIC TATTOO COMPANY

2518 Sunset Blvd
Silver Lake ⑫
+1 213 413 6530
*americanelectric
tattoocompany.com*

Founded in 1999 by Craig Jackman, who is famous for his portrait work and his sense of humor, this popular tattoo parlor recently moved to Silver Lake. From old-school traditional to single-needle portraits, they are proficient in every style and open seven days a week.

173 THE HONORABLE SOCIETY

8424 Santa Monica
Boulevard #B
West Hollywood ⑥
+1 323 654 2440
thehonorablesociety.com

This is a charming spot – a tattoo parlor where you might have a cup of tea. Among the many talented artists working here is Marco Cerretelli, who trained beneath Maurizio Fiorini, the Italian tattoo master. Cerretelli is known for his 'girl heads', and black and gray neo-traditionalism.

174 INK INK TATTOO

830 Lincoln Blvd
Venice ③
+1 310 314 7703
inkinktattoo.org

Opened in 1995 by Karina Mayorga, this small and bright space is one of the oldest female-owned tattoo studios in the US and has an all-women staff of artists. Mayorga's work is highly regarded; she especially likes doing black and gray portraits.

175 SHAMROCK SOCIAL CLUB

9026 W Sunset Blvd
West Hollywood ⑥
+1 310 271 9664
shamrocksocialclub.com

Mark Mahoney, the proprietor of this studio, is a legend and one of the most important tattoo artists in the world. His idiosyncratic career makes for lots of good stories, and his style is singular. Good luck trying to book him, though; his list of clients is long and includes many celebrities.

172 AMERICAN ELECTRIC TATTOO COMPANY

5 *items to*

CUSTOMIZE

---

176 GENERAL ADMISSION
GUY OKAZAKI
SURFBOARDS
52 Brooks Avenue
Venice ③
+1 310 399 1051
guyokazaki.com
generaladmission.us

Guy Okazaki has been surfing his whole life and shaping boards since the 1950s. He describes making custom surfboards as being a professional matchmaker – customers fall in love with their boards. If you are looking for a surfboard, this shop in Venice that has some of his boards is your first stop.

177 CACTUS STORE
PLANTS
1505 ½ Echo Park Ave
Echo Park ⑫
+1 213 947 3009
hotcactus.la

This narrow shop, opened by a team of cactus collectors, houses more than 450 rare and unique cacti that you can purchase – from a diminutive desk plant to a spiky wonder the size of a small child. Though it's a perfect souvenir of California, getting it home would certainly be prickly.

178 JACKIE ROBBINS
LEATHER GOODS

2522 W Magnolia
Boulevard
Burbank ⑭
+1 818 970 7720
jackierobbins.com

Specializing in custom handmade bags for men and women, as well as handcrafted jewelry (especially rosaries and rosary belts) designer Jackie Robbins will make sure you get a unique, one-of-a-kind accessory. She hand-stains and distresses the leather herself!

179 JAMES TRUSSART
GUITARS

1307 Allesandro St
Echo Park ⑫
+1 213 989 1554
jamestrussart.com

A musician-turned-luthier, Trussart crafts custom steel-bodied guitars, basses, and violins here at his home studio. The tones of his instruments are so distinctive they are used by legendary musicians such as Bob Dylan, Jack White, and Keith Richards.

180 LOT, STOCK AND BARREL
CHAIN STITCHING

8363 W 3rd Street
West Hollywood ⑥
+1 323 879 9896
lotstockandbarrel.com

This is the retail space of a full-service design studio. One of the many services they offer here is custom hand-done chain-stitch embroidery, a technique and art form that dates back to the late 1800s. From monograms to custom images, everything is done by hand.

50 BUILDINGS TO SEE

---

5 golden-era
MOVIE PALACES

---

181 EGYPTIAN THEATRE

6712 Hollywood Blvd
Hollywood ⑦
+1 323 461 2020
egyptiantheatre.com

This gem of a movie theater – still in operation as the American Cinematheque – is often overlooked by the hordes of tourists visiting the famous Chinese Theatre up the street. Like the Chinese, it was managed by impresario Sid Grauman, who staged elaborate performances for film premieres in the beautiful courtyard.

182 WARNER GRAND THEATRE

478 W 6th Street
San Pedro ⑰
+1 310 548 2493
grandvision.org

Now a thriving performing arts venue, this gorgeous, 1500-seat Art Deco movie theater still hosts film screenings as well. The same team that designed the Hollywood Pantages Theatre and Los Angeles City Hall built this historic landmark.

183 MILLION DOLLAR THEATRE

307 S Broadway
Downtown ⑩
+1 213 617 3600
milliondollar.la

Opened in 1918, this was Sid Grauman's (the legendary founder of Grauman's Chinese Theatre in Hollywood, now known as the TLC Chinese Theatres) first LA venue and one of the earliest (and largest) movie palaces in the US. It anchors the impressive Broadway Theatre District and is used as a special event and filming location today.

184 FOX VILLAGE THEATRE (REGENCY VILLAGE)

961 Broxton Avenue
Westwood ⑤
+1 310 208 5576
regencymovies.com

This Spanish Mission-style theater was opened in 1931; its tower is a Westwood landmark. Since then the 1400-seat theater has been a prestigious site for movie premieres. Across the street is the Bruin Theater, opened in 1937, so studios could run simultaneous screenings in both theaters for premieres.

185 VISTA THEATRE

4473 Sunset Blvd
Los Feliz ⑦
+1 323 660 6639
vintagecinemas.com/vista

Opened in 1923, the Vista boasts décor inspired by the discovery of King Tut's tomb in 1922. At his beloved neighborhood theater, manager Victor Martinez is famous for dressing in costume for film openings, and the sidewalk out front is a mini version of the Chinese Theatre's, with the handprints of locally loved film stars and directors.

183 EGYPTIAN THEATRE

The 5 greatest
GOOGIE-STYLE
buildings

---

186 CHIPS

11908 Hawthorne
Boulevard
Hawthorne ⑰
+1 310 679 2947

Googie is an architectural style popular in the mid-20th century and created in LA that captures the futurism of the time with buildings marked by aerodynamic lines, vaulted roofs, and gorgeous signage that played to the automobile age. Chips is a classic example of this popular style and has been in continuous operation since it opened in 1957.

187 NORMS RESTAURANT

470 N La Cienega
Boulevard
West Hollywood ⑥
+1 310 657 8333
normsrestaurants.com

This restaurant, designed by the influential architectural firm of Armet & Davis, exemplifies Googie style. It's also the oldest location of the Norms chain, which has locations around Southern California and is a quintessential California coffee shop.

188 PANN'S

6710 La Tijera Blvd
Inglewood ⑰
+1 323 776 3770
panns.com

Pann's is a perfect California coffee shop. Opened by George and Rena Panagopoulos in 1958 and designed by the legendary Armet & Davis, it's on the way to LAX so always a good way to say goodbye or hello to Los Angeles. The neon sign, like the fried chicken, is a thing of beauty.

189 JOHNIE'S COFFEE SHOP

6101 Wilshire Blvd
Miracle Mile ⑧
+1 323 938 3521

It's worth crossing Fairfax Avenue from the Los Angeles County Museum of Art to see this shuttered example of a Googie coffee house. Designed by Armet & Davis and opened in 1956, this space held a series of coffee shops before closing in 2000. Since then, the building has been used strictly as a film location.

190 JACK COLKER'S 76 STATION

427 N Crescent Drive
Beverly Hills ⑤
+1 310 273 3891

Googie was a popular style, not an elite one, so it's no wonder the finest examples are places of everyday experiences – coffee shops, gas stations, grocery stores. Architect William Pereira originally designed the swooping boomerang-shaped roof for LAX, but when it wasn't used there, he repurposed it here.

187 NORMS RESTAURANT

188 PANN'S

5 interesting buildings by
SCI-ARC ARCHITECTS

191 **SOUTHERN CALIFORNIA INSTITUTE OF ARCHITECTURE (SCI-ARC)**

960 E 3rd Street
Downtown/
Arts District ⑩
+1 213 613 2200
sciarc.edu

Founded in 1972 to provide a more experimental approach to architecture, SCI-Arc remains one of the few independent architecture schools in the world. A rehabilitated 100-year-old freight house serves as the school's campus. Outside, the 'League of Shadows' structure is an event pavilion built by students.

192 **HAYDEN TRACT**

Eight blocks
from Higuera St
to Jefferson Blvd,
between National
Blvd and the Los
Angeles River
Culver City ④
ericowenmoss.com

This former industrial zone now houses a concentration of innovative buildings designed by LA architect Eric Owen Moss, who served as the director of the Southern California Institute of Architecture (SCI-Arc) from 2002 to 2015.

192 HAYDEN TRACT

193 CALTRANS DISTRICT 7 HEADQUARTERS

151 E 1st Street
Downtown ⑩
morphosis.com

LA architect and one of SCI-Arc's founders, Thom Mayne and his Morphosis firm designed this futuristic building, which won the prestigious Pritzker Architecture Prize. It features a 'double skin' of glass behind perforated aluminum panels that can open and close based on the movement of the sun.

194 EMERSON COLLEGE LOS ANGELES

5960 Sunset Blvd
Hollywood ⑦
+1 323 498 0600
emerson.edu/la,
morphosis.com

Another futuristic work by architect Thom Mayne and Morphosis, this is the west coast campus for Boston's Emerson College. In a swirl of glass and steel, two residential towers connect to a sculptural base that houses lecture halls and production facilities for the college's film school.

195 FREDONIA APARTMENTS

3625 Fredonia Drive
Studio City ⑭
kappearchitects.com/
raykappe.html

Architect Ray Kappe designed this beautiful, elliptical-shaped apartment building in 1964. Along with being one of LA's most preeminent modern residential architects, Kappe is also an educator who helped found SCI-Arc.

5 former
OLYMPIC SITES

196 **ELYSIAN PARK**
929 Academy Road
Elysian Park ⑮
+1 213 485 5054
*laparks.org/park/
elysian*

The city's second-largest park and its oldest, Elysian is a treasure of natural wonders and breathtaking hikes. It's also the home of Dodger Stadium and the Los Angeles Police Department's training center. During the 1932 Olympics, held in LA, the police academy's pistol range was used for Olympic shooting competitions.

197 **LOS ANGELES MEMORIAL COLISEUM**
3911 S Figueroa St
Exposition Park ⑰
+1 213 747 7111
lacoliseum.com

Opened as a memorial to Los Angeles' World War I veterans, this has been the home of the USC Trojan football team since 1923. It hosted the Olympic Games in 1932 and 1984 and is currently the venue for the Rams professional football games. Historic tours are led around the Coliseum.

198 LA84 FOUNDATIONS/ JOHN C. ARGUE SWIM STADIUM

3980 Bill
Robertson Lane
Exposition Park ⑰
+1 213 763 0129
*laparks.org/expo/
aquatic*

Built for the 1932 Summer Olympics, this beautiful facility has hosted some of the best swimmers in the world. In fact, by 1970 some 65 world records were set at the stadium, more than anywhere else in the world. It is open to the public too.

199 MARINE STADIUM PARK

5255 Paoli Way
Long Beach ⑰
+1 562 570 3215
*longbeach.gov/park/
park-and-facilities/
directory/marine-
stadium*

This park offers one of the world's premier water-skiing facilities, along with a sand beach, rest rooms, and ample parking. This historic site hosted the 1932 Olympic rowing competition and the 1968 Olympic rowing trials. Today, rowing is allowed from sunrise to 8 pm.

200 THE FORUM

3900 W Manchester
Boulevard
Inglewood ⑰
+1 310 330 7300
fabulousforum.com

Reopened in 2014 after a revitalization that restored the signature red hue (called 'Forum Red') to the impressive 1967 building, the famed Forum is a premier – and historic – venue for concerts. Originally built to be a Taj Mahal for sports by the then-owner of the Lakers basketball team, the Forum's primary function was replaced by the Staples Center.

5 perfect examples of
PROGRAMMATIC ARCHITECTURE

---

201 BROWN DERBY DOME

3377 Wilshire Blvd
Koreatown ⑨

All that remains of the flagship restaurant of this famed Hollywood institution is a dome shape at the back of this strip mall. It's the ghost of the hat-shaped dome that was once a perfect example of what is called 'programmatic' architecture, a whimsical style wherein buildings were designed to resemble their function or wares.

202 THE DONUT HOLE

15300 Amar Road
La Puente ⑯
+1 626 968 2912
thedonuthole.net

Get ready for greatness because this bakery combines two of LA's iconic experiences: fresh donuts and drive-thru restaurants. A landmark since 1968, the Donut Hole is a drive-thru donut shop shaped like two donuts.

204 RANDY'S DONUTS

203 IDLE HOUR

4824 Vineland Ave
North Hollywood ⑭
+1 818 980 5604
idlehourbar.com

Reopened after a thoughtful restoration, this barrel-shaped restaurant and bar was built in 1941 as a taproom by a film tech from nearby Universal Studios – hence, the whiskey-barrel design. After time as a flamenco-dance showcase, it was saved by preservationists and restored by the 1933 Group, which operates the bar today.

204 RANDY'S DONUTS

805 W Manchester
Boulevard
Inglewood ⑰
+1 310 645 4707
randysdonuts.com

Another iconic building that is a donut shop – is there any doubt Angelenos love their donuts? Since 1953 Randy's has been welcoming visitors who spot the shop on the route from LAX because how could they miss it? There's a giant donut on top! Also seen in films such as *Iron Man II* and *Mars Attacks!*

205 THE TAMALE

6421 Whittier
Boulevard
East LA

Sadly for your stomach, this tamale-shaped structure is no longer serving tamales; presently, it's a salon and another business. But when it opened in 1928, it was a restaurant that served 'tamale pies', hence the distinctive architecture.

5

CASE STUDY
homes

———————

206 EAMES HOUSE (#8)
203 Chautauqua Blvd
Pacific Palisades ②
+1 310 459 9663
eamesfoundation.org

Make a reservation online before trying to visit this landmark of mid-century modern architecture, also known as Case Study House Number 8. Designed and constructed by Charles and Ray Eames, the couple lived in the house until their deaths. The house and the grounds are magical.

207 BAILEY HOUSE (#20)
219 Chautauqua Blvd
Pacific Palisades ②
+1 310 459 9663
eamesfoundation.org

While visiting the Eames House, be sure to look at the other homes you can catch glimpses of on the surrounding bluff. Five Case Study Houses were built here, including *Arts & Architecture* publisher John Entenza's house (#9) and this one by Richard Neutra, which is visible from the street and not open to the public.

208 CASE STUDY HOUSE #21
9038 Wonderland Park Avenue
West Hollywood ⑥

Architect Pierre Koenig designed this simple home, built of steel and glass, before he built his more famous Case Study House (#22). Tucked into the hill, it was completed in 1959 and remains one of the finest examples of Koenig's steel-frame houses.

209 STAHL HOUSE (#22)

1635 Woods Drive
West Hollywood ⑥
+1 208 429 1058
stahlhouse.com

The most recognizable of all the Case Study homes, no doubt because of photographer Julius Shulman's incredible portrait of it – if a single image could sum up modern architecture in Los Angeles, that would be it. The Pierre Koenig-designed home is open for tours, but be sure to book one before you go.

210 CASE STUDY HOUSE #16

1811 Bel Air Road
Bel-Air

From the street (which is the only way to view this stunning home), the Los Angeles Conservancy says this house looks like a 'glowing, floating glass pavilion'. It's certainly worth checking out Craig Ellwood's design, the only surviving Case Study by Ellwood that is still intact.

206 EAMES HOUSE (#8)

5

NEUTRAS

not to miss

---

211 EAGLE ROCK RECREATION CENTER

1100 Eagle Vista Dr
Eagle Rock ⑮
+1 323 257 6948
*laparks.com/reccenter/
eagle-rock*

Though he is mostly known for his residential design, this 1953 community center by Richard Neutra bears several of his signature motifs. The walls of the clubhouse can be opened up to the outdoors, so that parents watching their kids play basketball can do so beneath trees. Hardly a relic, it's a living testament to modernism's rich legacy.

212 NEUTRA VDL RESEARCH HOUSE

2300 Silver Lake Blvd
Silver Lake ⑫
neutra-vdl.org

This incredible multifamily residence is open for tours on Saturdays on a first-come, first-served basis (no reservations required). Originally built in 1932, this was Neutra's home until it was destroyed by fire in 1963. Dion Neutra, his son, rebuilt the house with his father's oversight.

213 OHARA HOUSE

2210 Neutra Place
Silver Lake ⑫
+1 323 666 1806
neutra.org

Built near Neutra's own home by the Silver Lake Reservoir, this gorgeous 1959 residence was named after its original Japanese owners. The home is part of what is often referred to as the Neutra colony, a collection of ten modernist homes all designed by the architect – the closest Neutra ever came to realizing his vision for a modernist townscape.

214 LOVELL HOUSE

4616 Dundee Drive
Los Feliz ⑪
+1 323 666 1806
neutra.org

Located next to Griffith Park and visible only through the trees, this is Neutra's famous International-style Lovell House. It is sometimes called the Lovell Health House because the owner Philip Lovell was a naturopath who commissioned the architect to make him a house that would improve the health of its inhabitants. Neutra delivered.

215 POPPY PEAK HISTORIC DISTRICT

Between La Loma
Rd (N), Ave 64 (E),
Poppy Peak Dr (S),
and the Pasadena
city limits (W)
Pasadena ⑬

This enclave in the winding hills of southwest Pasadena contains one of the finest concentrations of mid-century modern homes in Southern California, many built by prominent master architects of the style. Of course, there is a Neutra in the mix, visible from the street at 1540 Poppy Peak Drive.

The 5 most
ICONIC LA STRUCTURES

---

216 HOLLYWOOD SIGN

Griffith Park ⑪
hollywoodsign.org

Is it fitting that the most famous symbol of our fair city originated as an ad for a real estate development? Whatever the case, the sign, which originally read 'Hollywoodland', has been beckoning from Mount Lee in Griffith Park since 1923. In the 1970s, citizens and celebrities who sponsored each letter saved the sign.

217 GRAUMAN'S CHINESE THEATRE (TCL CHINESE THEATRES)

6925 Hollywood Blvd
Hollywood ⑦
+1 323 461 3331
tclchinesetheatres.com

Like the Hollywood Sign, this opulent theater is quintessential Hollywood. The vision of impresario Sid Grauman, who managed the theater until the 1950s, the Chinese opened in 1927. For decades, film stars have been cementing their handprints in concrete at the theater's famous Forecourt of the Stars.

218 THEME BUILDING AT LAX

209 World Way
Westchester ⑰
lawa.org

This space-age icon is known worldwide. Opened in 1961 and designed by the prestigious firm Pereira and Luckman, the mid-century modern building looks like a UFO landed in the middle of LAX. For decades, a fine-dining restaurant was located here; today the building is vacant.

219 BRADBURY BUILDING

304 S Broadway
Downtown ⑩
+1 213 626 1893
thebradbury.com

Built in 1893, this landmark building is the oldest commercial building in the central city and is instantly recognizable to anyone who's seen *Blade Runner,* provided you go inside. There, the five-story central courtyard is flooded with natural light from the ceiling skylight, and the elaborate wrought iron and birdcage elevators are breathtaking.

220 WATTS TOWERS

1765 E 107th Street
Watts ⑰
+1 213 847 4646
wattstowers.org

Though less well known than other iconic LA structures, this dream-like complex of spiraling steel towers covered with mortar and hand-tiled mosaics captures the visionary spirit of the city. Built by Simon Rodia from 1921 until 1955, the towers remain a testament to the power of imagination and the persistence of vision.

218 THEME BUILDING AT LAX

5 locations from
UNSUNG TV SERIES

221 6TH STREET BRIDGE & THE LOS ANGELES RIVER

E 6th Street
Downtown ⑩
+1 213 923 0586
the6thstreetbridge.com

Currently under construction. Architect Michael Maltzan is redoing this iconic bridge crossing the Los Angeles River. The concrete banks beneath the bridge are often used as locations for commercials, as well as TV shows and films such as *Them* and *Terminator 2: Judgment Day*.

222 ECHO PARK LAKE

751 Echo Park Ave
Echo Park ⑫
+1 213 847 0929
laparks.org/aquatic/
lake/echo-park-lake

Built in 1868 as a drinking reservoir, this area is now a popular park for locals. The recreational lake, which grows incredible lotus flowers, features paddle boating, a great cafe in the boathouse, and a fantastic view of downtown LA. This is where the Keystone Cops chased each other in their madcap celluloid adventures.

223 LINDA VISTA COMMUNITY HOSPITAL

610-630 S St. Louis St
Boyle Heights ⑩

Opened in 1905 by the Santa Fe Railway as a hospital for its employees, this Mission-style building was recently revitalized and transformed into housing for seniors. Before that it was reputed to be one of the city's most haunted locales. For decades, the abandoned hospital was a popular filming site *(True Blood* and many TV shows).

224 PALACE THEATRE

630 S Broadway
Downtown ⑲
+1 213 488 2009
palacedowntown.com

One of many historic movie palaces located on Broadway, this 2000-seat theater first opened as a vaudeville house in 1911; Sarah Bernhardt, Harry Houdini, and the Marx Brothers all performed here. For decades, it has been used as a film location, including for Michael Jackson's *Thriller* video and as the offices of Olivia Pope on *Scandal*.

225 SANTA ANITA PARK

285 W Huntington Dr
Arcadia ⑯
+1 626 574 7223
santaanita.com

This beautiful and historic Art Deco-style racetrack has long been a popular filming location. Of course, the 2003 film *Seabiscuit* was shot here – the real Seabiscuit lived and trained here. Also, many TV shows such as *Alias, Bones,* and *Grey's Anatomy* have made use of its pristine period locales.

222 ECHO PARK LAKE

5 ways to get inside

ARCHITECTURAL HOMES

226 **THE GAMBLE HOUSE**
4 Westmoreland Pl
Pasadena ⑬
+1 626 793 3334
gamblehouse.org

This incredible example of Arts and Crafts-style architecture was designed by Pasadena architects Charles and Henry Greene in 1908. One-hour tours are available Thursday through Sunday, but a great way to get a quick glimpse is 'Brown Bag Tuesday', where you can lunch on the terrace and take a 20-minute docent-led tour.

227 **GREYSTONE MANSION**
905 Loma Vista Drive
Beverly Hills ⑤
+1 310 285 6830
greystonemansion.org

The 18-acre grounds of the former Doheny Estate are now a park and open every day. The opulent mansion at its center, the former 55-room home of Edward 'Ned' Laurence Doheny (who was found shot dead in the house only five months after moving in) is open only for special events through the Friends of Greystone.

228 **HOLLYHOCK HOUSE**
4800 Hollywood Blvd
Hollywood ⑦
+1 323 913 4030
barnsdall.org

Frank Lloyd Wright's first project in LA was a home built for oil heiress Aline Barnsdall and was completed in 1921. The center of the Barnsdall Art Park, the residence – named for Barnsdall's favorite flower, a design motif incorporated into the house – is open for tours Thursday through Sunday.

229 LUMMIS HOUSE

200 E Avenue 43
Highland Park ⑬
+1 213 485 4833
laparks.org/historic/
lummis-home-and-
garden

Charles Fletcher Lummis built this incredible stone house, also known as El Alisal, in the late 1890s. Lummis, a historian, reporter, and Native American rights activist, entertained prominent guests including John Muir, Will Rogers, and Clarence Darrow at his home. It is open for the Lummis Festival in June.

230 SCHINDLER HOUSE

835 N Kings Road
West Hollywood ⑥
+1 323 651 1510
makcenter.org

Home of the MAK Center for Art and Architecture, the Schindler House is open Wednesday through Sunday. Regarded as a masterpiece of modern architecture, the 1922 home was conceived by Rudolf Schindler and his wife, Pauline, as an experiment in communal living; it was the epicenter of social gatherings for many influential thinkers.

228 HOLLYHOCK HOUSE

GRIFFITH OBSERVATORY

100 THINGS
TO DISCOVER

———

The 5 best
URBAN HIKES

---

231 ARROYO SECO
AT: ARROYO SECO
FOUNDATION
570 W Ave 26 #450
Pasadena ⑮
+1 323 405 7326
arroyoseco.org

The beautiful Arroyo Seco watershed snakes down from the San Gabriel Mountains through Pasadena, South Pasadena, and Northeast Los Angeles to the confluence with the Los Angeles River near Elysian Park. There are many different hikes to try covering all kinds of terrain, from urban gritty walks by whizzing freeways to trails in pristine canyons.

**232 BALDWIN HILLS
SCENIC OVERLOOK**
6300 Hetzler Road
Culver City ④
+1 310 558 5547
www.parks.ca.gov

This 500-foot peak is southwest of downtown Los Angeles and offers a short hike to a panoramic view of the entire Los Angeles Basin, the Pacific Ocean, and the surrounding mountains. The native habitat has been restored, so you can envision what LA was like before any of us got here.

233 GRIFFITH PARK
4730 Crystal
Springs Drive
Griffith Park ⑪
+1 323 913 4688
laparks.org/griffithpark

One of the most stunning features of LA is this mostly undeveloped parkland in the middle of the city, where in minutes you can be among rugged hills and wild animals. There's a network of 53 miles of hiking trails here; maps are available online and at the ranger station.

234 RUNYON CANYON PARK

2000 N Fuller Avenue
West Hollywood ⑥
+1 213 485 5572
laparks.org/park/
runyon-canyon

Wear something cute to hike here because as far as natural excursions go, this one is a Hollywood scene. There are three entrances to this hillside public facility, a long stretch of terrain from Mulholland Drive to Fuller Avenue. The views of the city are incredible, but you might be distracted by celeb sightings too.

235 VISTA HERMOSA PARK

100 N Toluca Street
Downtown ⑩
+1 213 250 1100
lamoutains.com

Few folks even know this hidden gem of a park exists, which allows visitors to enjoy the 10 acres of walking trails, play space, and spectacular skyline views of nearby downtown. Formerly developed land, this space in the city's urban core has been given back to nature.

235 VISTA HERMOSA PARK

5 incredible
ETHNIC ENCLAVES

---

236 **CAMBODIA TOWN**
Anaheim St
betw Atlantic Ave
and Junipero Ave
Long Beach ⑰
cambodiatown.com

Los Angeles is one of the most ethnically diverse cities in the world; its multiculturalism is a large part of the city's dynamism, and citizens take great pride in their polyglot culture. Long Beach has the largest concentration of Cambodians outside of Cambodia, and the 1,2-mile stretch of businesses celebrates and strengthens the community.

237 **LITTLE ARMENIA**
Betw Vermont Ave
and the 101 Freeway
from Hollywood Blvd
to Santa Monica Blvd
Hollywood ⑦
littlearmenia.com

Once home to the largest population of Armenian people outside of Armenia, this area of East Hollywood has a concentration of Armenian restaurants, markets, bakeries, and other services. It is also home to significant Thai and Latin populations.

238 **LITTLE TEHRAN/
PERSIAN SQUARE**
Westwood Blvd
betw Wilshire Blvd
and Pico Blvd
West LA

A pocket of Persian restaurants and shops came into being after the Iranian Revolution in 1979, when many Iranians fled Iran and immigrated to Los Angeles. Today, LA has the largest population of Persians outside of Iran, earning it the moniker Tehrangeles or Little Tehran.

239 LEIMERT PARK VILLAGE

Betw Exposition
Blvd, South Van Ness
Ave and Arlington
Ave, West Vernon
Ave, and Victoria Ave
and Crenshaw Blvd
Leimert Park ⑰
leimertparkvillage.org

Since the 1950s, this quaint community of tree-lined streets has been one of the largest black middle-class neighborhoods in the US. Filmmaker John Singleton once called it 'the black Greenwich Village' for the vibrancy of its arts community. One trip to Leimert Park Village, home of Eso Won Bookstore, and you'll understand why.

240 SAWTELLE JAPANTOWN (LITTLE OSAKA)

Betw Santa Monica
Blvd and Pico Blvd,
from Centinela Ave
to the 405 Freeway
West LA

Since the 1930s, this area has been home to a sizable Japanese American population; many of the early settlers were Japanese gardeners who purchased land here to open nurseries. This thriving community was uprooted, and many of its citizens interned, during World War II. Today, Japanese restaurants and businesses once again thrive.

240 SAWTELLE JAPANTOWN

5 famous
CULT LOCATIONS

241 THE AETHERIUS SOCIETY

6202 Afton Place
Hollywood ⑦
+1 323 465 9652
aetherius.org

LA has long been a center of spiritual exploration and fringe beliefs. Since 1965 this site, enclosed by a pink fence with cosmic art on its gates, has been the headquarters of the group started by George King, a man who was contacted by an extraterrestrial named 'Aetherius' that gave him a series of advanced teachings.

242 THE PEOPLES TEMPLE

1366 S Alvarado St
Downtown ⑩

Not all of the alternative religions in LA are positive ones – though the headquarters for Jim Jones' Peoples Temple was in Northern California. In the early 1970s they began having services here, eventually setting up a staff and recruiting new members.

243 SCIENTOLOGY CELEBRITY CENTRE INTERNATIONAL

5930 Franklin Ave
Hollywood ⑦
+1 323 960 3100
scientology.cc

This building was originally the Chateau Elysee, a luxury apartment building and hotel that was a frequent haunt of film stars. These glory days were long gone when Scientology purchased it in 1973 and restored its glamour so that they could cater to artists, politicians, and people with 'power and vision'.

244 SYMBIONESE LIBERATION ARMY/ LAPD SHOOTOUT

1466 E 54th Street
Vernon ⑰

One of the city's most infamous shootouts took place on this site on May 17, 1974, when a police SWAT team exchanged fire with members of the Symbionese Liberation Army – the group that kidnapped heiress Patty Hearst and killed Dr. Marcus Foster. The standoff lasted two hours, and six SLA agents were killed.

245 UNIFICATION CHURCH RECRUITMENT CENTER (NOW THE ALCOVE RESTAURANT)

1929 Hillhurst Ave
Los Feliz ⑦

Before this building became a popular brunch restaurant, it was once a recruitment center for the Unification Church. Mocked as the 'Moonies', the members of the church followed the teachings of the Reverend Sun Myung Moon, a self-proclaimed messiah who presided over mass marriages.

The 5 most
HAUNTED SITES

246 EL PUEBLO DE LOS ANGELES

125 Paseo de la Plaza
Downtown ⑩
+1 213 628 1274
elpueblo.lacity.org

The city started here and so do its ghosts. The Pico House, a luxury hotel built in 1870, is said to be haunted by the ghosts of people who were hung in trees on what once was the town square. Also, the victims of the 1871 Chinese Massacre are said to haunt the area.

247 HOUDINI MANSION

2398 Laurel Canyon
Blvd (now 2400
Laurel Canyon Blvd)
Laurel Canyon ⑥
+1 323 886 4949
thehoudiniestate.com

This secluded property was across the street from a house that was once rented by the great magician and later became the home of his widow, Bess. A tunnel existed under Laurel Canyon that connected their small house to a mansion built here, where Bess held séances to summon her husband.

248 KNICKERBOCKER BUILDING

1714 Ivar Avenue
Hollywood ⑦

Once a luxury hotel with a glamorous nightclub, the Knickerbocker was another place where Bess Houdini held a séance every Halloween. Here director D.W. Griffith had a stroke, and in 1962 a woman jumped from a hotel window to her death. These unfortunate events are said to inspire paranormal activity at the site.

249 COLORADO STREET BRIDGE

504-532 W Colorado
Boulevard
Pasadena ⑬
nps.gov/nr/travel/
*route66/colorado_*
*street_bridge_*
pasadena.html

When it was built in 1913, this beautiful
bridge was the largest concrete bridge in
the world; today it is known as the 'suicide
bridge'. The first suicide happened in 1919;
since then estimates are that more than
100 people have ended their lives here.
Their ghosts are said to haunt the area.

250 SILENT MOVIE THEATRE

611 N Fairfax Avenue
Fairfax ⑧
+1 323 655 2510

On January 17, 1997, the owner of this
theater, Laurence Austin, was shot and
killed during a film screening. Evidence
revealed the shooter was a contract killer
hired by Austin's lover – and the theater's
projectionist – James Van Sickle. Austin's
ghost is said to haunt the theater.

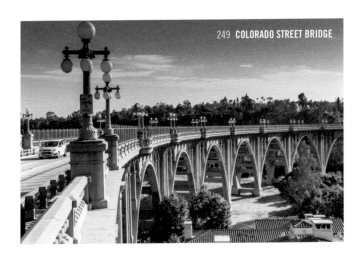

249 COLORADO STREET BRIDGE

5 places to see on the
SUNSET STRIP

251 RAINBOW BAR AND GRILL

9015 W Sunset Blvd
West Hollywood ⑥
+1 310 278 4232
*rainbowbarand
grill.com*

Before it became a frequent hangout for rock musicians in the 70s and 80s, this was the site of a restaurant owned by film director Vincente Minnelli. It became the Rainbow Room in 1972 and opened, fittingly, with a party for Elton John. Today, it's a living reminder of what the Sunset Strip once was.

252 THE ROXY THEATRE

9009 W Sunset Blvd
West Hollywood ⑥
+1 310 278 9457
theroxy.com

In 1973, a group of prominent record producers (Lou Adler, David Geffen, Elliot Roberts, Peter Asher) came together with nightclub owner Elmer Valentine to create the kind of music venue they wanted – the Roxy. Neil Young opened the club, kicking off decades of great performances.

253 WHISKY A GO GO

8901 W Sunset Blvd
West Hollywood ⑥
+1 310 652 4202
whiskyagogo.com

Like the Roxy, one of the most important rock clubs in LA, this still vital venue hosted pretty much every great act you can think of from the 1960s and 70s (The Byrds, the Kinks, the Who), and the 80s and 90s (X, Guns N' Roses).

254 THE VIPER ROOM

8852 W Sunset Blvd
West Hollywood ⑥
+1 310 358 1881
viperroom.com

Johnny Depp opened The Viper Room in 1993; although he's no longer attached, it's still got his rock 'n' roll vibe. Throughout the 90s, it was the go-to place, drawing folks like Johnny Cash, Tom Petty, Flea, and Steve Jones to its stage. Actor River Phoenix died of a drug overdose on the sidewalk outside the club in 1993.

255 SITE OF SCHWAB'S PHARMACY

8024 Sunset Blvd
West Hollywood ⑥

This legendary drug store had a paging service so that agents could reach the actors hanging out there, and the owners of the shop extended credit to the non-working among them. The most famous stars in Hollywood mingled with the nobodies, and everyone was welcome – it was democracy at its best!

251 RAINBOW BAR AND GRILL

The 5 most interesting
WALKING TOURS

256 LOS ANGELES CONSERVANCY

523 W 6th St #826
Downtown ⑩
+1 213 623 2489
laconservancy.org

The nonprofit Los Angeles Conservancy is the largest preservation group of its kind and the group responsible for safeguarding many of the city's most treasured historic places. The group's knowledgeable docents host weekly walking tours focused on specific styles (Art Deco) or areas (downtown's historic core, the Broadway Theatre District).

257 FELIX IN HOLLYWOOD

STARTS AT: 1500 VINE ST
Hollywood ⑦
+1 323 363 4668
felixinhollywood tours.com

Led by a Hollywood historian and former costume supervisor, this two-hour walking tour takes you back (to 1910!) to the origins of the major film studios, the radio and TV networks, and record companies that made Hollywood hallowed ground and the capital of the entertainment industry.

258 SANTA MONICA CONSERVANCY

2520 2nd Street
Santa Monica ②
+1 310 496 3146
smconservancy.org

Every Saturday this preservation organization hosts a two-hour walking tour (comprising only of six blocks) that retraces Santa Monica's history from its Wild West days to how it became the vibrant community it is today.

259 NOHO HISTORIC WALKING TOUR

STARTS AT: MUSEUM OF THE SAN FERNANDO VALLEY

18860 Nordhoff
Street #204
Northridge ⑭
+1 818 347 9665
themuseumsfv.org

This small museum boasts an interesting collection of materials about unsung aspects of the Valley's history. They also sponsor occasional walking tours that give patrons a firsthand experience of the Valley's past. Themes of tours include celebrity homes, haunted sites, and an exploration of Van Nuys.

260 VINTAGE VENICE

STARTS AT: 1601 MAIN ST

Venice ③
+1 424 999 8687
vintagevenicetours.com

Jonathan Kaplan takes you backwards in time on his fantastic walking tours of Venice, starting with the dreamer Abbot Kinney and his vision of 'Venice of America'. Sharing film clips and other memorabilia along the way, Kaplan captures the beauty and the funk of this area from Muscle Beach to Silicon Beach.

260 VINTAGE VENICE

5 beautiful
BOTANICAL GARDENS

261 THE ARBORETUM

301 N Baldwin Ave
Arcadia ⑯
+1 626 821 3222
arboretum.org

The first thing you might notice here has nothing to do with the botanicals – it's the peacocks that flaunt their stuff by the entrance. They fit into this unique and wonderful 127-acre garden that includes all kinds of plants, plus Native American, Rancho Period, and late-19th-century treasures.

262 DESCANSO GARDENS

1418 Descanso Drive
La Cañada
+1 818 949 4200
descansogardens.org

Once a ranch owned by Elias Boddy, who used much of his 165 acres to house his camellia collection, this land was purchased by Los Angeles County in 1952 (in part to prevent Walt Disney from buying it). Today it is an idyllic natural setting with stunning collections of a variety of plants.

263 THE HUNTINGTON

1151 Oxford Road
San Marino ⑯
+1 626 405 2100
huntington.org

A horticulturalist friend of mine describes this 120-acre private botanical collection as 'the Disneyland of Gardens', for the sheer glee it provokes from plant people. But even those uninterested in horticulture will find something of interest among the twelve different spectacular gardens.

264 SOUTH COAST BOTANIC GARDEN

26300 Crenshaw Boulevard
Palos Verdes ⑰
+1 310 544 1948
southcoastbotanicgarden.org

It's hard to believe that this beautiful 87-acre garden was once a sanitary landfill. A masterpiece of land reclamation, the collection includes a Garden for the Senses that encourages visitors to touch and smell the plants and flowers and a Children's Discovery Garden, so it's a perfect place for families.

265 VIRGINIA ROBINSON GARDENS

1008 Elden Way
Beverly Hills ⑤
+1 310 550 2068
robinsongardens.org

Built in 1911, this historic estate was once the residence of the Robinson family of the Robinson department store. It's exactly what you hope to experience in Beverly Hills – a world of privilege, luxury, and beauty. Along with expansive gardens, there's a mansion and pool pavilion to explore.

263 THE HUNTINGTON

5

SPORTS

to see

---

266 BEACH BOCCE BALL LEAGUE
MEET AT: PARKING LOT OF ON THE WATERFRONT CAFÉ
205 Ocean Front Walk
Venice ③
bocceleague.com

The beach is the perfect place to play bocce. Why not join in with this league that meets every Tuesday during the season (Memorial Day to Labor Day) to compete on Venice's sandy beach? Sign up online before you come to play.

267 LOS ANGELES DERBY DOLLS
MEET AT: THE DOLLOSEUM
4900 Alhambra Ave
Alhambra ⑮
derbydolls.com

This is an all-female, banked-track roller-derby league that is incredible to watch – the women are fast, tough, and inspiring. And the names of the teams and the players are such clever wordplays, you'll be clapping for them based on name alone.

268 LOS ANGELES VELODROME RACING ASSOCIATION
18400 Avalon Blvd
Carson ⑰
lavelodrome.org

Have you ever seen track cycling? This velodrome – an arena for track cycling – has steeply banked tracks on which riders speed by. It's impressive to watch and looks like fun to try.

269 VANS US OPEN OF SURFING

Huntington Beach
Pier
Huntington Beach ⑰
*vansusopenof
surfing.com*

Held every July, this nine-day celebration of surfing and surf culture brings together more than 300 world-class athletes – the best surfers in the world come to compete in the world's only surf arena. Also, there are competitions in skateboarding and BMX. Other entertainment includes outdoor film screenings, bands, and autograph sessions.

270 WILL ROGERS POLO CLUB

1501 Will Rogers
State Park Road
Pacific Palisades ②
+1 818 509 9965
willrogerspolo.org

This beautiful park was the private estate of Will Rogers, and this was his polo field until his wife gifted the estate to the state in 1935. In the 1930s, there were more than 25 polo fields in LA; this is the last one. The season runs from May until September.

5 fun attractions in
GRIFFITH PARK

---

271 AMIR'S GARDEN

A half-mile hike up the fire road near the Mineral Wells Picnic Area parking lot Griffith Park ⑪ *amirsgarden.org*

For 32 years, Amir Dialameh worked with a pick and shovel to create this incredible oasis in the midst of the park. He planted pine and jacaranda trees along with shrubbery to create a five-acre shady wonderland in what was previously a scorched landscape (fires are a problem in Griffith Park).

272 LA EQUESTRIAN CENTER

480 West Riverside Dr Burbank ⑪⑭ +1 818 840 9063 *la-equestriancenter.com*

This 75-acre facility feels very rural and provides a taste of the old West. It's a popular filming location and also a place where you can rent a horse for a ride through the stunning hills of Griffith Park.

273 OLD ZOO

4801 Griffith Park Dr Griffith Park ⑪ +1 323 913 4688 *laparks.org/griffithpark*

In 1966, the Los Angeles Zoo moved to its current location on 133 acres in the park, but many relics of the old zoo remain here, which was its location prior to the move. At this popular urban ruin in the midst of an idyllic setting, the old large-animal grottos have been transformed into picnic areas.

274 VERMONT CANYON TENNIS COURTS

2715 N Vermont
Canyon Road
Griffith Park ⑪
+1 323 664 3521
laparks.org/sports

Located not far from Griffith Park's Greek Theatre, this public tennis facility is a gorgeous place to play a game. With twelve courts built into the canyon, you are surrounded by nature-hiking trails, hills of chaparral, and the golf course below. There's a small charge to use the courts at certain times.

275 WALT'S BARN

5202 Zoo Drive
Griffith Park ⑪
+1 310 213 0722
carolwood.com/walts-barn/

Some say this little barn is the birthplace of Disney's Imagineering. Part of a miniature railroad Walt Disney created at his home in the 50s, the barn served as Disney's machine shop. Disney's daughter preserved the barn, and it is on loan to the city as part of the Los Angeles Live Steamers Museum.

5 *unusual*
SPA TREATMENTS

---

276 THE SOUNDBATH CENTER

4688 Eagle Rock Blvd
Eagle Rock ⑮
+1 323 839 6251
sound-bath.com

Soundbaths use gongs (sometimes tuned to the celestial bodies) and crystal singing bowls to create music that people bathe in while laying on their backs. It is supposed to promote deep relaxation, altered states of consciousness, and healing. This center offers private sessions or group soundbaths.

277 EXHALE SPA

AT: FAIRMONT MIRAMAR
HOTEL & BUNGALOWS

101 Wilshire Blvd
Santa Monica ②
+1 310 319 3193
exhalespa.com

Located in the tony Fairmont Miramar Hotel, this spa offers a variety of wellness practices such as cupping, reiki, and acupuncture. Their craniosacral massage involves light holding of the skull and sacrum with a series of barely detectable movements that have health benefits.

278 OLYMPIC SPA

3915 W Olympic Blvd
Koreatown ⑨
+1 323 857 0666
olympicspala.com

One of many Korean spas in Koreatown, this is one of the few that is open to women only. Many other spas offer the ritual of an *akasuri* body scrub, where someone vigorously scrubs away all the dead skin cells on your body, but the 'Pure Bliss' treatment here is, well, pure bliss.

279 THE SALT STUDIO

1380 E Walnut Street
Pasadena ⑬
+1 626 765 6180
saltstudiopasadena.com

Patrons come to this small studio in Pasadena for salt therapy, recommended to treat respiratory problems, colds, skin diseases, stress, and fatigue. This therapy consists of sitting in one of two tranquil salt rooms, one for adults and the other with activities for children.

280 WI SPA

2700 Wilshire Blvd
Koreatown ⑨
+1 213 487 2700
wispausa.com

This mega spa in Koreatown has something for everyone, including families – there's a huge co-ed *jimjilbang,* a communal space with a restaurant, lounge, and game room. The facilities are open 24 hours a day, so it's also popular for people recovering in the early morning hours from the prior night's indulgences.

279 THE SALT STUDIO

5

FILM STUDIO

tours to take

---

281 HOLLYWOOD HERITAGE MUSEUM

2100 N Highland Ave
Hollywood ⑦
+1 323 874 4005
hollywoodheritage.org

The nonprofit organization Hollywood Heritage oversaw the restoration and preservation of this 1901 structure, the Lasky-DeMille Barn, which was the actual building where director Cecil B. DeMille had his office, and his studio staff worked and played. Today, the barn houses the Hollywood Heritage Museum; the organization also offers walking tours of Hollywood.

282 PARAMOUNT PICTURES

5515 Melrose Avenue
Hollywood ⑦
+1 323 956 1777
paramount studiotour.com

The only major film studio left in Hollywood, Paramount is housed on a lot that has been part of movie-making history for more than 100 years. Thank goodness they offer three different tours, so you can see what lies behind the famous gates Norma Desmond drove through.

283 SONY PICTURES TOUR

10202 W Washington Boulevard
Culver City ④
+1 310 244 8687
sonypictures studiostours.com

There are many daily tours of the studio here – which in some ways is the real center of the golden era of Hollywood, not Hollywood, because this was the home to juggernaut MGM. Tours today visit the soundstage where iconic films such as *The Wizard of Oz* and *Singin' in the Rain* were made.

284 UNIVERSAL STUDIOS HOLLYWOOD

100 Universal City Plaza
Universal City ⑭
+1 800 864 8377
universalstudios hollywood.com

Of course, the rides at this theme park are amazing, especially since the Wizarding World of Harry Potter opened. Film lovers adore the studio tram tour for its glimpses of the back lot – it's a ride through filmmaking history from the people who initiated the business of film tourism.

285 WARNER BROS. STUDIO TOUR

3400 W Riverside Dr
Burbank ⑭
+1 877 492 8687
wbstudiotour.com

Often regarded as the best of the studio tours for its balance between showmanship and educational insights: this tour also does a nice mix of old and new film locations. Also recommended: getting tickets for one of the shows filming on the WB lot, so you can witness more behind-the-scenes action.

The 5
BEST VIEWS
of the city

---

286 GRIFFITH OBSERVATORY

2800 E Observatory Road
Griffith Park ⑪
+1 213 473 0800
griffithobservatory.org

You know this view – it's one that's often used to capture the city's vastness and its twinkling lights at night. But just because you've seen it in photos doesn't mean you won't be breathless with the city's magnitude and beauty in person. Watching the sunset is required.

287 OBSERVATION DECK AT LOS ANGELES CITY HALL

200 N Main Street
Downtown ⑩
+1 213 473 3231
lacity.org

For years, City Hall was the tallest building in LA. That changed in 1964, but the view from the building's observation deck on the 27th floor is still incredible. There's a 360-degree view of the Santa Monica Mountain range, the downtown skyline, and, on a clear day, Santa Monica and the Pacific Ocean.

288 ANGELS POINT IN ELYSIAN PARK

Angels Point Road
Elysian Park ⑮
+1 213 485 5054
laparks.org

You can get to this stunning vista in Elysian Park one of two ways: drive up the remote Angels Point Road and find a place to park on the side of the curvy road, or take a rugged 3-mile hike through the park. Either way, the result is a bird's-eye view of the downtown skyline.

289 SKYSLIDE AT U.S. BANK TOWER

633 W 5th St #840
Downtown ⑲
+1 213 894 9000
oue-skyspace.com

This view experience is the polar opposite of Angels Point. You will not be left solitary to savor the view among singing birds; instead you are, with many others, on California's tallest open-air observation deck. The unobstructed view is stunning, but if that isn't enough thrill for you, try the glass slide.

290 HILLTOP PARK

2351 Dawson Avenue
Signal Hill ⑰
+1 562 989 7330
cityofsignalhill.org

Signal Hill is a small enclave surrounded entirely by Long Beach. At the top is this park, which has views of the Santa Monica Mountains, downtown LA, Griffith Park, Long Beach, and all the communities in between. Plus, you can see down the South Bay to Newport Beach and across the sea to Catalina Island.

5

METRO STOPS

to stop at

---

291 PICO (CHICK HEARN) STATION
BLUE LINE
1236 S Flower Street
Downtown ⑩
+1 323 466 3876
metro.net

LA's metro system is one of the best-kept secrets – some visitors don't even know the city has a rail system. We do, plus much more as far as public transport goes. The best way to get to the Staples Center is to go Metro and use this station, named for the famed Lakers' announcer.

292 DOWNTOWN SANTA MONICA STATION
EXPO LINE
401 Colorado Avenue
Santa Monica ②
+1 323 466 3876
metro.net

This is it, the eagerly awaited western terminus of the Expo Line, a light-rail line that goes from downtown Los Angeles to downtown Santa Monica. When it opened in 2016, it was the first time in a generation that Angelenos could travel by train to the beach.

293 MARIACHI PLAZA STATION
GOLD LINE
1831 E 1st Street
Boyle Heights ⑩
+1 323 466 3876
metro.net

This stop in Boyle Heights is named for Mariachi Plaza, the city's center of mariachi culture where musicians would gather. On weekends, music can often be heard coming from the plaza's traditional *quiosco,* which was a gift from the Mexican state of Jalisco – the birthplace of mariachi.

294 **HOLLYWOOD/ HIGHLAND STATION**
RED LINE
6801 Hollywood Blvd
Hollywood ⑦
+1 323 466 3876
metro.net

This station for the underground subway Red Line is in the heart of Hollywood; upon exiting the station you are on Hollywood Boulevard, with all of the major tourist attractions easily walkable (Grauman's Chinese Theatre, the Dolby Theatre, Musso & Frank).

295 **UNION STATION**
PURPLE LINE
800 N Alameda St
Downtown ⑲
+1 323 466 3876
metro.net

The beginning of the Purple Line subway is the venerable Union Station. When the line is complete in 2023, it will traverse parts of downtown, Koreatown, Hollywood, Fairfax, West Hollywood, Beverly Hills, and Westwood.

293 MARIACHI PLAZA STATION

The 5 most interesting
SECRET STAIRWELLS

---

296 BROADVIEW TERRACE STAIRS

High Tower Drive &
Los Altos Place
Hollywood ⑦
secretstairs-la.com

Throughout LA, stairways thread and connect hillside communities to the streets below. Built by early developers and municipal city planners, these stairs allowed people who lived in hillside residences to reach businesses, schools, and public transport lines. If you are a fan of the film version of Raymond Chandler's *The Long Goodbye,* you must visit here.

297 BAXTER STAIRS

2100 Park Drive
Echo Park ⑮
secretstairs-la.com

This might be the best workout in town with no gym fees to pay. One of the longer staircases, this 231-step climb goes from the bottom of Baxter Street up into Elysian Park, offering stunning views along the way of the downtown skyline and the hills of Hollywood and Glendale.

298 THE MATTACHINE STEPS

2355 Cove Avenue
Silver Lake ⑫
secretstairs-la.com

These stairs are named in honor of the gay rights organization the Mattachine Society, founded in 1950 by Harry Hay, who lived in a nearby house at 2328 Cove Avenue. A memorial to this pioneering force in the gay rights movement, the stairs offer a stunning view of the Silver Lake Reservoir below.

299 MUSIC BOX STEPS

923 N Vendome St
Silver Lake ⑫
secretstairs-la.com

Three blocks off Sunset Boulevard, these are the stairs made famous by the 1932 Laurel and Hardy film *The Music Box*. In the short film, the bumbling comic duo try to carry a piano up the long stairwell.

300 SANTA MONICA STAIRS

699 Adelaide Drive
(betw 4th and 7th St)
Santa Monica ②
secretstairs-la.com

Fitness fans love this set of two stairways – one wooden, one concrete – that are each equal to climbing about eight flights of stairs. Most folks utilize both sets of stairs, running up the wooden and down the concrete or vice versa. And then we hope they take a nap on the beach below.

5 things
LOVED BY LOCALS

301 **ANGELS FLIGHT**

351 S Hill Street
Downtown ⑩
angelsflight.org

This is the little funicular that could! The shortest railway in the world, this 116-year-old funicular takes passengers up and down Bunker Hill between Hill and Olive Streets. Originally opened in 1901, the two iconic orange cars closed in 2013 due to an accident, but thankfully the historic railway reopened in the fall of 2017.

302 **MONASTERY OF THE ANGELS' PUMPKIN BREAD**

1977 Carmen Avenue
Hollywood ⑦
+1 323 466 2186
monasteryof theangels.org

Only the gluten-intolerant among us can turn away from the loaves of pumpkin bread sold in the gift shop of this Roman Catholic convent. Made by the Dominican nuns who live cloistered here, all sales from the small shop support the sisters.

301 ANGELS FLIGHT

303 SELF-REALIZATION FELLOWSHIP LAKE SHRINE TEMPLE

17190 Sunset Blvd
Pacific Palisades
+1 310 454 4114
lakeshrine.org

While this area was once a film studio (it was first the silent-era Inceville, then a part of 20th Century Fox), today this is one of the most peaceful spots in the city. Owned by the Self-Realization Fellowship, the ten acres include a temple, a shrine, and a meditation garden – and are open to the public.

304 FERN DELL

Fern Dell Drive
Griffith Park ⑪
*laparks.org/
griffithpark/poi*

Through the Western Avenue entrance, you will find an enchanted bit of Griffith Park known as Fern Dell (sometimes spelled Ferndell). There's a shady trail that snakes along a creek, marked by faux bois rails and wooden bridges built in the 1930s by the Conservation Corps. It's a haven during the heat.

305 VENICE CANALS

START AT: CORNER
OF WASHINGTON BLVD
AND STRONGS DR
Venice ③

There are canals still existent in Venice, but so hidden they are easy to miss – but don't, because these three canal-lined blocks give you a totally different take on the beach community. There's even a launch ramp should you have brought your own kayak, and outdoor movies in the summer.

5 of the most unlikely
PLACES TO
SEE CELEBS

---

306 BEACHWOOD MARKET

2701 Belden Drive
Hollywood ⑦⑪
+1 323 464 7154

This quaint, family-owned grocery store is a convenient stop while exploring the area around the Hollywood Sign. It's also a good place to shop if you live nearby without having to traipse down the hill. Odds are you won't see big A-list stars here, but you might spot someone from TV picking up a gallon of milk.

307 SANTA MONICA FARMERS' MARKET

Arizona Ave
(at 2nd St)
Santa Monica ②
smgov.net/
farmersmarket

If the types of celebrities you're interested in seeing are the ones on Food Network, then this is the place. This outdoor market held on Wednesdays is a long-standing date for most of LA's premier chefs – many of them, of course, have television shows.

308 JOAN'S ON THIRD

8350 W 3rd Street
West Hollywood ⑥
+1 323 655 2285
joansonthird.com

This cafe, with ample outdoor and communal seating, draws people of all kinds together thanks to its central location. Whether you are at a table or shopping the gourmet market, be sure to look at more than just the food – this unpretentious and delicious cafe is a good place to spot a star being nondescript.

309 **LARCHMONT VILLAGE WINE & CHEESE**

223 N Larchmont Boulevard
Hollywood ⑦
+1 323 856 8699
larchmontvillage wine.com

This neighborhood offers a pedestrian-friendly strip of boutiques, restaurants, and specialty shops (donuts! coffee! books!). Folks in the know come to this wine shop for the incredible sandwiches, so don't be surprised if you see someone you recognize from TV splitting some turkey and prosciutto ones with friends.

310 **WHOLE FOODS 365**

2520 Glendale Blvd
Silver Lake ⑫
+1 323 378 3891
365bywholefoods.com

This hip grocery store in cool Silver Lake has some of the best prices in town on organics, which maybe explains why the edgier celebs are spotted here (their careers aren't huge, they've got to be thrifty and chic!). I once saw several cast members from *Girls* getting goods for a house party.

310 WHOLE FOODS 365

5

RODARTE FAVORITES

---

311 **THE HUNTINGTON LIBRARY, ART COLLECTIONS, AND BOTANICAL GARDENS**

1151 Oxford Road
San Marino ⑯
+1 626 405 2100
huntington.org

Rodarte, the luxury fashion label founded by sisters and LA natives Kate and Laura Mulleavy, mixes high couture with laidback California influences. One of the designers' favorite places is the 120-acre Huntington Gardens, which has a stunning collection of twelve different gardens and one of the largest collections of camellias in the world.

312 **CARAVAN BOOKSTORE**

550 S Grand Avenue
Downtown ⑲
+1 213 626 9944

This antiquarian bookstore is musty and mysterious in the most romantic of ways – it's a reminder of how the printed word can transport us to worlds unknown. In business for more than 60 years, the store has a selection of rare and secondhand books that will inspire wonder.

313 **NORTON SIMON MUSEUM**

411 W Colorado Blvd
Pasadena ⑬
+1 626 449 6840
nortonsimon.org

Founded in 1922 as the Pasadena Art Institute, this charming art museum has collections of European art, Asian sculpture, and wood-block prints. One of its van Gogh paintings inspired Rodarte's 2012 clothing line. This museum was the first US museum to show retrospectives of Duchamp and Warhol.

314 MOUNT WILSON OBSERVATORY

AT: ANGELES NATIONAL FOREST
La Cañada ⑯
+1 323 654 7100
mtwilson.edu

Not far up the 2 Freeway from where the designers grew up in Pasadena, this historic observatory located at the peak of the San Gabriel Mountains also inspired Rodarte's 2012 collection – specifically, sunspots seen from the telescope. Visit for a weekend tour and see where the Milky Way galaxy was first measured.

315 TOWER BAR

AT: SUNSET TOWER HOTEL
8358 W Sunset Blvd
Sunset Strip ⑥
+1 323 848 6677
sunsettowerhotel.com

The Mulleavy sisters have mentioned that this cozy restaurant inspired by early Hollywood is one of their favorite places to go. Located in a 1931 landmark Art Deco building on the Sunset Strip, this is classic LA – both Frank Sinatra and John Wayne once lived here.

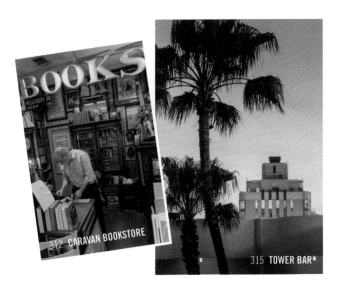

312 CARAVAN BOOKSTORE

315 TOWER BAR

5

CLASSIC CAR SHOWS

---

316 BOB'S BIG BOY

4211 W Riverside Dr
Burbank ⑭
+1 818 843 9334
bobs.net

The action for car-design aficionados starts on Friday afternoons as a selection of gleaming classic cars pull into the parking lot vying for spaces – it's like a scene from the film *American Graffiti,* with shiny classic cars, a Googie-style diner, and carhops. The hoods are opened up and while those in the know admire the handiwork, the rest of us ogle and enjoy, sipping milkshakes.

317 EARLY RODDERS

AT: UNITED ARTISTS
THEATRE
1919 Verdugo Blvd
La Cañada ⑰

Early on Saturday mornings, the parking lot outside this movie theater serves as the scene for vintage cars and hot rods. Mostly members of the local car club, folks peer under the hoods and exchange shop talk over coffee. The action begins around 6.30 am and ends by 8.30, so come early and have the freeways all to yourself.

318 MID CITY CAR MEET

5746 W Adams Blvd
Mid City ④

Car shows aren't just about the vehicles, although that's certainly the point for most of the people who attend them. For the rest of us, they're a slice of Americana. The weekly meeting of this club on Wednesdays includes a cruise and is open to all.

319 ODD SQUAD CAR CLUB COFFEE CRUISE

9829 Venice Blvd
Culver City ④
oddsquadcc.com

This club, which has no requirements other than that your car be a pre-smog American car (that's before 1976), meets weekly on Wednesdays from 7 to 9 pm. Introduce yourself to members and enjoy checking out their cars in the Coffee Bean parking lot.

320 CARS & CRUISE

16882 Gothard St, Unit A
Huntington Beach ⑰
+1 714 831 1888
hbhotrodnews.com

Designed for hot rod, custom, classic, and vintage car enthusiasts and their fans, this group meets Wednesday evenings from 6.30 till 8.30 pm. Founded by Mel Craig, the event also has an online news network.

316 BOB'S BIG BOY

5 great
NEON SIGNS

---

321 MUSEUM OF NEON ART

216 S Brand Blvd
Glendale ⑮
+1 818 696 2149
neonmona.org

The only museum in the world devoted exclusively to neon, this beautiful museum showcases electric and kinetic art and historic neon sign preservation. The collection includes the famous Brown Derby rooftop sign from the restaurant's Hollywood & Vine location.

322 CIRCUS LIQUOR

5600 Vineland Ave
North Hollywood ⑭
+1 818 769 1500
circusliquor.com

You've maybe seen this 32-foot-tall neon clown before. When Cher gets mugged in the film *Clueless,* she's standing in front of it. Since 1960, the clown has towered over Burbank Boulevard, shining like a beacon for those seeking the Valley's number-one-rated liquor store.

323 HELMS BAKERY

8758 Venice Blvd
Culver City ④
+1 310 204 1865
helmsbakerydistrict.com

Today this design complex lights up Venice Boulevard with a relic from the building's history as an industrial bakery. Before it closed in 1969, Helms' fresh-baked bread was a staple in the Southland; it was also the official bread of the 1932 Olympic Games. The animated neon sign that shines on harkens back to that history.

324 BROADWAY THEATRE DISTRICT

3rd to 9th Streets
along South
Broadway
Downtown ⑩

This is the first and largest historic theater district listed on the National Register of Historic Places and a great concentration of grand movie theaters and their fabulous neon-drenched marquees. Efforts from several preservation organizations have restored many of the theaters and relit the gorgeous neon signs.

325 WESTLAKE THEATRE

638 S Alvarado Street
Westlake ⑩

Perched atop this beautiful 1926 movie theater is a three-story neon sign announcing its name to the city below. It's a marker for the neighborhood and though the building has been under rehabilitation for years, the sign is unlit. Still, it is impressive.

The 5 most interesting
ARCHITECTURE & DESIGN TOURS

---

326 AIA/LA TOURS

3780 Wilshire
Boulevard #800
Koreatown ⑨
+1 213 639 0777
aialosangeles.org

Who better to conduct a tour than a bunch of architects? The Los Angeles chapter of the American Institute of Architects offers small groups monthly tours of very specific sites such as particular buildings or neighborhoods. These popular tours sell out fast.

327 ARCHITECTURE TOURS L.A.

START AT VARIOUS
LOCATIONS
+1 323 464 7868
architecturetoursla.com

In an air-conditioned mini-van, an architectural historian and author takes patrons around particular areas of town – Silver Lake, Downtown, Pasadena – or on tours of the works of specific architects such as Frank Gehry and Frank Lloyd Wright.

328 THE CENTER FOR LAND USE INTERPRETATION

9331 Venice Blvd
Culver City ④
+1 310 839 5722
clui.org

The bus tours run by this organization do not go to the usual locales; instead, there might be a tour of on-site office trailers at construction sites or a behind-the-scenes look at the Los Angeles Department of Water and Power's electrical supply center. They've even done tours to the dump, all to explore the meaning of contemporary landscapes.

329 CHARLES PHOENIX

charlesphoenix.com

Gain an appreciation for Los Angeles' landmarks and unique design aesthetic on author and entertainer Charles Phoenix's curated tours. This 'Ambassador of Americana' covers a dizzying array of subjects, from architecture and history to mom-and-pop shops and the best snacks stops. Often riding on a vintage yellow school bus, he will take you back in time.

330 ESOTOURIC

3001 N Broadway
Downtown ⑩
+1 213 373 1947
esotouric.com

The most creative tour company in town, these folks are experts in the most fascinating and esoteric (get it?) parts of LA's diverse history. Hop on the bus for one of their in-depth true crime (Hotel Horrors) or literary tours (James M. Cain and the Birth of Noir, Bukowski's LA). They know lost Los Angeles like no one else.

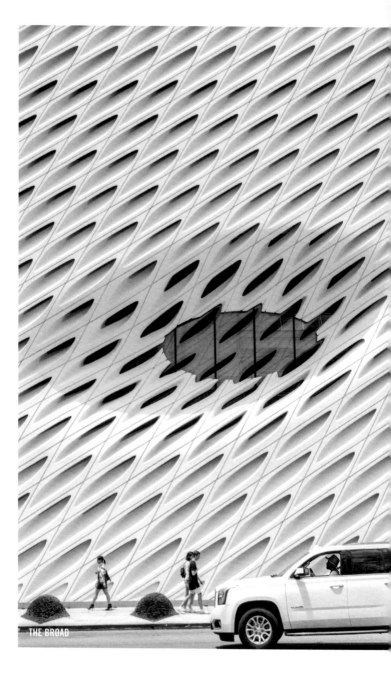

THE BROAD

55 WAYS TO ENJOY CULTURE

5
PRIVATE COLLECTIONS
open to the public

---

331 THE BROAD
221 S Grand Avenue
Downtown ⑲
+1 213 232 6200
thebroad.org

This new contemporary art museum,
founded by philanthropists Eli and
Edythe Broad, opened in 2015. The
museum (designed by the same architects
behind New York's High Line) houses
2000 works from their collection,
which is heavy on contemporary artists
including Cindy Sherman, Ed Ruscha,
and Jeff Koons. Yayoi Kusama's 'Infinity
Mirrored Room' is magical.

332 FREDERICK R. WEISMAN ART FOUNDATION
265 N Carolwood Dr
Hombly Hills ⑤
+1 310 277 5321
weismanfoundation.org

Philanthropist Frederick Weisman
purchased this 1920s estate to house
his personal collection of 20th-century
art, including works by Cezanne, Picasso,
Magritte, Rauschenberg, Rothko, and
Ruscha. Overseen by the Weisman
Art Foundation, this collection of more
than 400 works is open to the public
by appointment only for guided tours.

333 MARCIANO ART FOUNDATION

4357 Wilshire Blvd
Central LA ⑨
+1 424 204 7555
*marcianoart
foundation.org*

This collection of contemporary art from the 1990s to the present is owned by Maurice and Paul Marciano (founders of the GUESS brand). Entry is free (though reservations are required), and the building itself is of interest; it's a former Scottish Rite Masonic Temple built by Millard Sheets in 1961.

334 NETHERCUTT COLLECTION

15200 Bledsoe Street
Sylmar/San
Fernando Valley ⑭
+1 818 364 6464
nethercuttcollection.org

Founded by the car-obsessed nephew of the founder of Merle Norman Cosmetics, the Nethercutt showcases more than 130 beautifully restored antique and classic automobiles. The museum itself is modeled after an opulent 1920s automobile salon, making this an immersive time-travel experience.

335 VINCENT PRICE ART MUSEUM

AT: EAST LOS ANGELES
COLLEGE
1301 Cesar Chavez Ave
Monterey Park ⑯
+1 323 265 8841
*vincentprice
artmuseum.org*

This museum located on the campus of East Los Angeles College houses the collection of actor Vincent Price – whose interest in art was enthusiastic and far-reaching – and includes works from Africa, Europe, Mesoamerica, and the indigenous people of North America. Price's sizable donation inspired others, and today the museum has a collection of more than 8000 works.

5

ART SCHOOLS

that changed the art world

---

336 ARTCENTER COLLEGE OF DESIGN

1700 Lida St #2319
Pasadena ⑬
+1 626 396 2200
artcenter.edu

Since the mid-20th century Los Angeles has been a center of the art world, and some of the most radical movements and most groundbreaking works of art happened here. Art schools, which supported working artists and trained new ones, had a role in creating that vibrancy. Opened in 1930, ArtCenter follows a conservatory approach to this day.

337 CALIFORNIA INSTITUTE OF THE ARTS (CALARTS)

24700 McBean
Parkway
Valencia
+1 661 255 1050
calarts.edu

Envisioned by Walt Disney as a multi-disciplinary community where future generations of artists could be nurtured by working artists instead of academics, Disney and his brother merged two existing art schools into CalArts in 1961. Who knew his utopia would be the breeding ground for artists like Tim Burton, Mike Kelley, Guillermo Gómez-Peña, and Carrie Mae Weems?

338 SITE OF CHOUINARD ART INSTITUTE

763 Grand View St
Westlake
chouinard
foundation.org

Founded in 1921, Chouinard was a training ground for Disney animators – it's said that Walt himself would drive his employees to classes here. Later, Disney, in gratitude for the service the school had provided his studio (Mary Blair and Ed Benedict studied here), began financially supporting the school and merged it into CalArts.

339 SITE OF THE WOMAN'S BUILDING

1727 N Spring Street
Chinatown ⑩
laconservancy.org/
locations/womans-
building

For 18 years (1973–1991), this building was at the center of feminist art practices in LA, and many of the artists working here changed the art world forever. Founded by female artists who routinely found their work (and their bodies and lives) marginalized, this cooperative space became a beehive of feminist activity and creativity.

340 OTIS COLLEGE OF ART AND DESIGN

9045 Lincoln Blvd
Westchester ⑰
+1 310 665 6800
otis.edu

Named for the *Los Angeles Times* publisher who donated his home to become an art school in 1916, Otis was the largest art school west of Chicago by 1922. Notable teachers throughout the school's history include Millard Sheets, Peter Voulkos, and Sheila de Bretteville. It continues to offer interdisciplinary education in the arts.

5 historic
HIP-HOP SITES

---

341 KENDRICK LAMAR'S CHILDHOOD HOME

1612 W 137th Street
Compton ⑰

The rapper and seven-time Grammy Award winner (and he'll get more) once lived in this three-bedroom house; as this is a private home, please don't disturb the current residents. Throughout his work, Lamar evocatively recalls his childhood growing up in Compton, from happily riding his bike down the street to witnessing a murder.

342 'LET ME RIDE' VIDEO LOCATION

W Slauson Ave and
Crenshaw Blvd
South LA ⑰

The music video for Dr. Dre's 1992 hit 'Let Me Ride' was shot on location in South Los Angeles, much of it along Slauson Avenue. If you don't remember it, here's a reminder: everyone is in it – Dre, Snoop Dogg, even Ice Cube.

343 SITE OF DEATH ROW RECORDS

10900 Wilshire
Boulevard #1240
Westwood ⑤

Founded in 1991 by music mogul Suge Knight and rapper and record producer Dr. Dre, Death Row was one of hip-hop's most influential and profitable labels until a series of internal problems (including the murder of Tupac Shakur and Knight serving prison time) led it to file for bankruptcy in 2006.

344 PETERSEN AUTOMOTIVE MUSEUM

6060 Wilshire Blvd
Miracle Mile ⑧
+1 323 930 2277
petersen.org

In 1997, rapper Notorious B.I.G., aka Biggie Smalls, was leaving a music-industry event held here when he was gunned down in his car. He was only 24 years old; the murder has never been solved, although many theorize it was in retaliation for the death of Tupac six months earlier.

345 SITE OF V.I.P. RECORDS

1030 Pacific Coast Highway
Long Beach ⑰
+1 562 591 2349
worldfamous viprecords.com

This one-time record shop is seminal in the history of hip-hop. Long-time owner Kelvin Anderson opened the store in 1978 and oversaw the transition from R&B to rap – in fact, he contributed to it by installing a recording studio in the shop, which is where Snoop Doggy Dogg, Warren G, and Nate Dogg recorded their demo. The rest is history.

344 PETERSEN AUTOMOTIVE MUSEUM

EXPERIMENTAL CINEMA

screenings

---

346 **ECHO PARK FILM CENTER**
1200 N Alvarado St
Echo Park ⑫
+1 213 484 8846
echoparkfilmcenter.org

This nonprofit media-arts organization is the neighborhood cinema of old Italian films – it's a place to discover the magic of movies and the people who make them. With a focus on empowering marginalized communities to create their own media, the center offers free educational programs and an eco-friendly mobile cinema.

347 **FILMFORUM**
AT: THE EGYPTIAN THEATRE
6712 Hollywood Blvd
Hollywood ⑦
lafilmforum.org

It's possible to see the most famous film in the world at the same theater where you can find the most experimental, non-commercial work. That's because Filmforum, Southern California's longest-running screening organization for independent and progressive media, makes its home at the Steven Spielberg Theatre here.

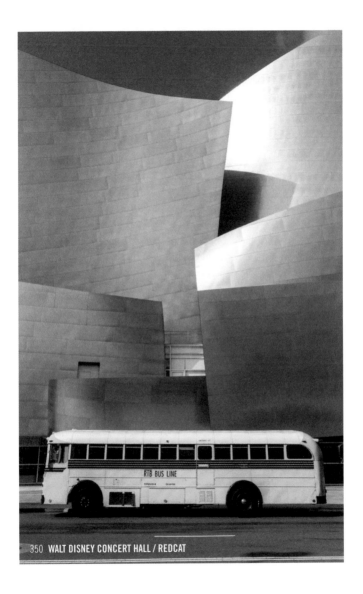

350 WALT DISNEY CONCERT HALL / REDCAT

348 BILLY WILDER THEATER

AT: HAMMER MUSEUM
10899 Wilshire Blvd
Westwood ⑤
+1 310 206 8013
cinema.ucla.edu

This shockingly-hot-pink theater, named for the great film director, is the home of the UCLA Film & Television Archive's public programs, which vary from classic film to more experimental fare. Along with contemporary, independent films from around the world, the theater also screens holdings from the archive's vast holdings – in their original formats.

349 NEW BEVERLY CINEMA

7165 Beverly Blvd
Fairfax ⑧
+1 323 938 4038
thenewbev.com

This is LA's most legendary repertory theater; since 1978 it's been a haven for movie lovers with nightly double features of classic and art-house films. In 2014 film director Quentin Tarantino, a loyal patron, purchased the theater. He now serves as head programmer, and many of the film prints come from his collection.

350 ROY AND EDNA DISNEY/CALARTS THEATER (REDCAT)

631 W 2nd Street
Downtown ⑩
+1 213 237 2800
redcat.org

This interdisciplinary arts center located inside the Walt Disney Concert Hall complex has an ambitious film and video program that screens some of today's most adventurous filmmakers and media artists. Special events include festivals and works that combine film and video with live performance. There's a gallery and bar too.

5 great
OBSCURE MUSEUMS

---

351 LOS ANGELES POLICE MUSEUM

6045 York Boulevard
Highland Park ⑮
+1 323 344 9445
laphs.org

Anyone with an interest in popular culture will find this museum dedicated to the history of the Los Angeles Police Department interesting. Attractions include armored cars, a prison cell, and artifacts from some of the LAPD's major incidents, including rooms devoted to the SLA and North Hollywood shootouts.

352 CRAFT & FOLK ART MUSEUM

5814 Wilshire Blvd
Miracle Mile ⑧
+1 323 937 4230
cafam.org

This museum, near LACMA, highlights the intersections of craft, art, and design and introduces visitors to a group of diverse makers and artists. Plus, there's often an interactive element to their exhibitions and programs, such as hands-on workshops with practitioners. Also, there's a great gift shop.

353 PASADENA MUSEUM OF CALIFORNIA ART

490 E Union Street
Pasadena ⑬
+1 626 568 3665
pmcaonline.org

This area of Pasadena, the Playhouse District, houses several important museums (the USC Pacific Asia Museum is nearby). This one, devoted to California artists, is a great way to explore the rich cultural mix and influences that make California unique.

354 **THE MUSEUM OF JURASSIC TECHNOLOGY**
9341 Venice Blvd
Culver City ④
+1 310 836 6131
mjt.org

A truly unique experience, this museum will have you scratching your head in wonder. There are unlikely exhibitions, such as a gallery of oil paintings of cosmonaut dogs or intricately carved fruit stones. Enjoy complimentary tea and cookies in the Tula Tea Room.

355 **VELVETERIA**
711 New High Street
Chinatown ⑩
+1 626 714 8545
velveteria.com

At a flea market nowadays one can spend hours searching for a black velvet painting; here you can enjoy a collection of more than 450 velvet paintings. Though you can't take any of them home, curators and owners Caren Anderson and Carol Baldwin will make you feel right at home here.

354 THE MUSEUM OF JURASSIC TECHNOLOGY

5 cultures
BORN IN LA

---

356 ALOUD
AT: CENTRAL LIBRARY
630 W 5th Street
Downtown ⑩
+1 213 228 7500
*lfla.org/calendar/
category/aloud*

The biggest literary stars come to share and discuss their books at this series offered by the Library Foundation of Los Angeles. Held in the beautiful 1926 Central Library, these conversations, readings, and performances are free to the public but do require advance reservations.

357 CICLAVIA
VARIOUS LOCATIONS
525 S Hewitt Street
Downtown/
Arts District ⑩
+1 213 355 8500
ciclavia.org

One of the best ways to explore LA, CicLAvia is a quarterly event that temporarily closes streets to car traffic and opens them to people – you can walk, bike, skate, or dance through the streets of LA. The neighborhoods for events are always changing, so check the website for news.

358 CINESPIA
AT: HOLLYWOOD
FOREVER CEMETERY
6000 Santa Monica
Boulevard
Hollywood ⑦
cinespia.org

This organization hosts outdoor film screenings in the Hollywood Forever Cemetery, one of the oldest cemeteries in LA and final resting place of Johnny Ramone, Rudolph Valentino, and Jayne Mansfield. Patrons can bring picnics and watch classic films in a unique – oddly beautiful – setting.

359 HAMMER MUSEUM

10899 Wilshire Blvd
Westwood ⑤
+1 310 443 7000
hammer.ucla.edu

What started as a museum for the collections of Dr. Armand Hammer is now a dynamic space for exploring art and ideas. Along with exhibitions of art (including the biennial 'Made in LA' show), the Hammer hosts film screenings and public programs that bring together influential writers, artists, and creative thinkers.

360 THE MAGIC CASTLE

7001 Franklin Ave
Hollywood ⑦
+1 323 851 3313
magiccastle.com

Only LA has the talent pool to sustain a private club for professional magicians. Founded by Milt Larsen in 1963, this mansion is the clubhouse of the Academy of Magical Arts, and every night some of the best magicians in the world perform here – exclusively for other magicians. Guests must be invited or accompanied by a member.

358 CINESPIA

5 cultural sites in the
SAN FERNANDO VALLEY

---

361 GREAT WALL OF LOS ANGELES
12900 Oxnard Street
North Hollywood ⑭
sparcinla.org

This half-mile-long mural along the Tujunga Flood Control Channel is a pictorial history of the ethnic people of California from prehistoric times to the mid-20th century. Conceived by artist Judy Baca, it was completed in the 1970s with more than 400 youth and their families participating in its creation.

362 MURAL MILE
13520 Van Nuys Blvd
Pacoima ⑭
+1 818 570 3570
muralmile.org

One of the best concentrations of murals in the city, the three miles of Van Nuys Boulevard surrounding Pacoima City Hall feature more than 50 murals, many of which portray the area's history. Artist and Pacoima native Levi Ponce contributed more than a dozen of these murals, created with a crew of collaborators.

362 **MURAL MILE**

363 LEONIS ADOBE MUSEUM

23537 Calabasas Rd
Calabasas
+1 818 222 6511
leonisadobemuseum.org

Built in the 1870s, this was the home of Miguel Leonis, a sheep rancher and real estate investor who owned a large portion of the western San Fernando Valley at the time. Today, his former estate is a historical monument with a museum that explores and preserves California ranch life in the 1880s.

364 VALLEY PERFORMING ARTS CENTER

18111 Nordhoff Street
Northridge ⑭
+1 818 677 3000
*valleyperforming
artscenter.org*

This 1700-seat theater on the campus of California State University in Northridge offers multidisciplinary performances that feature performers and artists from around the world. The idea is to appeal to all of LA's rich and diverse communities; check the schedule because they do!

365 VALLEY RELICS MUSEUM

21630 Marilla Street
Chatsworth ⑭
+1 818 678 4934
valleyrelicsmuseum.org

Open to the public with free admission only on Saturdays, this collection of historical artifacts pertaining to the San Fernando Valley is vast and worth saving a weekend afternoon for. There are vintage neon signs, photographs, clothing, cars, and even bicycles, all of which tell the history of the Valley's rich past.

5 places to explore
ANCIENT LA

---

366 LA BREA TAR PITS AND MUSEUM

5801 Wilshire Blvd
Miracle Mile ⑧
+1 213 763 3499
tarpits.org

No matter how hot it gets in LA, the ice age is never far away. At the center of our city are the bubbling La Brea Tar Pits, one of the world's most famous fossil localities, where the remains of saber-toothed cats, dire wolves, and mammoths have been uncovered.

367 NATURAL HISTORY MUSEUM

900 Exposition Blvd
Exposition Park ⑰
+1 213 763 3466
nhm.org

There's so much more than dinosaurs here (although both the Dino Lab and the interactive Dinosaur Encounters are pretty cool). Along with a Butterfly Pavilion, a Spider Pavilion, and a hands-on Nature Lab, there's the 'Becoming LA' exhibit, which explores how the modern city came to be. The First Friday events are especially fun.

368 HISTORIC SOUTH-WEST MUSEUM

234 Museum Drive
Mount Washington ⑮
+1 323 221 2164
theautry.org/visit/mt-washington-campus

Now part of the Autry Museum, this museum was created by Charles Fletcher Lummis in early 1914 as a place to exhibit one of the world's finest collections of Native American artifacts. Today, the historic building serves as the Autry's Mount Washington outpost and is open on Saturdays.

369 ORCUTT RANCH HORTICULTURAL CENTER

23600 Roscoe Blvd
West Hills
+1 818 346 7449
*laparks.org/
horticulture/orcutt-
ranch*

This ranch was the retirement home of William Warren Orcutt, who discovered one of the first prehistoric skeletons at the La Brea Tar Pits. Among the 240 acres of gardens there are oak trees here estimated to be more than 700 years old. For one weekend in July the orchards are open for public picking.

370 ZANJA MADRE

AT: LOS ANGELES STATE
HISTORIC PARK
1245 N Spring Street
Downtown ⑩
+1 323 441 8819
lashp.com

This fantastic 13-acre state park at the northern end of downtown is a former rail yard transformed into green space with wonderful public art. It's also the site where in 1759 Spanish forces forded the Los Angeles River and created the Zanja Madre, or 'Mother Ditch', the city's first aqueduct.

366 LA BREA TAR PITS AND MUSEUM

The 5 best
OUTDOOR CONCERT
venues

---

371 GREEK THEATRE

2700 N Vermont Ave
Griffith Park ⑪
+1 844 524 7335
lagreektheatre.com

Smaller and more hidden than the Hollywood Bowl, this outdoor amphitheater in Griffith Park opened in 1930. During World War II, the Greek was used for army barracks. Now the 5900-seat venue hosts big-time musical performers and smaller community events such as school concerts and graduations.

372 GRAND PERFORMANCES

AT: CALIFORNIA PLAZA
Two California Plaza,
350 S Grand Avenue
Downtown ⑩
+1 213 687 2190
grandperformances.org

This amazing series of free performing arts programs and concerts lasts all summer long and brings some of the biggest talent to public space. It's a global roster of performers with everyone from Stevie Wonder to Hamed Nikpay.

373 STARLIGHT BOWL

1249 Lockheed
View Drive
Burbank ⑭
+1 818 238 5397
starlightbowl.com

Built in 1950, the best part of this smaller outdoor amphitheater is its great view of the mountains and its grassy lawn for lazy picnicking and lounging while you listen to a variety of family-friendly entertainment acts.

374 HOLLYWOOD BOWL

2301 N Highland Ave
Hollywood ⑦
+1 323 850 2000
hollywoodbowl.com

This is the largest natural outdoor amphitheater in the US, and many would argue the best outdoor concert venue in the world. Along with being the summer home of the Los Angeles Philharmonic, this historic and beloved icon hosts world-class musicians from all genres, classical to rock, reggae to hip-hop.

375 LEVITT PAVILION IN MEMORIAL PARK

85 E Holly Street
Pasadena ⑬
+1 626 683 5300
*levittpavilion
pasadena.org*

Located in historic Memorial Park, this 1930 band shell looks like a miniature Hollywood Bowl and hosts free concerts – jazz, blues, world, Latin, and children's music – throughout the summer season. Funded by the Levitt Foundation, the idea is for live music to bring people together and invigorate communities.

The 5 most important
THEATER COMPANIES
to see

---

376 **THE ACTORS' GANG**
9070 Venice Blvd
Culver City ④
+1 310 838 4264
theactorsgang.com

Guided by actor Tim Robbins, who is the founding artistic director of the company, the Actors' Gang has produced more than 200 plays in Los Angeles. Working out of this historic building – an old railroad power station – the respected company continues to present groundbreaking and entertaining plays.

377 **CENTER THEATRE GROUP**
VARIOUS VENUES
601 W Temple
Street (office)
Downtown/
Little Tokyo ⑩
+1 213 628 2772
centertheatregroup.org

Operating in three theatres – the Ahmanson Theatre, the Mark Taper Forum, and the Kirk Douglas Theatre – and under the direction of Michael Ritchie, this is one of the US's most influential nonprofit theater companies. For 50 years, they have presented a mix of celebrated shows, classic plays, and adventurous new works.

378 DEAF WEST THEATRE

5112 Lankershim
Boulevard
North Hollywood ⑭
+1 818 762 2998
deafwest.org

Founded by deaf actor Ed Waterstreet in 1991, this venue is home to an acclaimed theater company of, by, and for the deaf. Productions integrate English and American Sign Language (ASL) with signing actors rather than having an ASL interpreter to the side.

379 THE FOUNTAIN THEATRE

5060 Fountain Ave
Hollywood ⑦
+1 323 663 1525
fountaintheatre.com

This nonprofit organization has a small theater in Hollywood where it prioritizes multi-ethnic theater and dance, helping to develop new works or explore new takes on established plays that speak to the concerns of a culturally diverse Los Angeles. Also, it hosts a year-round season at an affordable ticket price.

380 INDEPENDENT SHAKESPEARE COMPANY

4801 Griffith Park Dr
Griffith Park ⑪
+1 818 710 6306
iscla.org

Held in the summer at the site of Griffith Park's Old Zoo, this company's Griffith Park Free Shakespeare Festival brings the bard's classic works to a modern audience. Plays are preceded by pre-show performances by a variety of local artists, and families are welcome to attend. All events are free.

5 must-visit
GALLERIES

---

381 BERGAMOT STATION
2525 Michigan Ave
Santa Monica ②
+1 310 453 7535
bergamotstation.com

Named for the Red Line trolley line
that once had a stop here, this group
of warehouse buildings was transformed
in 1994 from industrial use to a complex
of art galleries. Now it's a destination for
art lovers who can spend a day browsing
the galleries.

382 CHINA ART OBJECTS GALLERIES
6086 Comey Avenue
Culver City ④
+1 323 965 2264
chinaartobjects.com

Opened in Chinatown in 1999, this gallery
helped usher in the multidisciplinary era
of art practice where artists, musicians,
writers, and designers cross over and
collaborate. Always pro-artist, the gallery
championed young artists and has grown
as their careers have into an establishment.
It moved to Culver City in 2010.

383 MACHINE PROJECT
1200D N Alvarado
Echo Park ⑫
+1 213 483 8761
machineproject.com

Like Human Resources, this is less
a traditional gallery than a space for
exploration that collaborates with artists,
thinkers, and the local community
to create projects. It's a nonprofit,
educational institution with a roster
of interesting and innovative events.

384 HUMAN RESOURCES (HRLA)

410 Cottage Home St
Chinatown ⑩
+1 213 290 4752
humanresourcesla.com

An artist-run gallery in Chinatown, Human Resources is a nonprofit project space for performance art and musical collaborations, as well as more traditional displays of art. A collaborative process organizes shows, and the gallery is meant to function as a resource for artists, rather than an institution or shop to sell their work.

385 LOS ANGELES CONTEMPORARY EXHIBITIONS (LACE)

6522 Hollywood Blvd
Hollywood ⑦
+1 323 957 1777
welcometolace.org

Founded in 1978 by artists, LACE was a pioneering exhibition space for artists working in then emergent art forms such as performance art, video art, and installations. Dedicated to promoting challenging and socially engaging work, artists the 40-year-old gallery championed include Mike Kelley, John Baldessari, Bill Viola, Adrian Piper, and Gronk early in their careers.

381 BERGAMOT STATION

ANNENBERG COMMUNITY BEACH HOUSE

20 THINGS TO DO
WITH CHILDREN

———

The 5 most fun
THEME PLAYGROUNDS

---

386 CULVER CITY PARK

9910 Jefferson Blvd
Culver City ④
+1 310 253 6650
culvercity.org/enjoy/
culver-city-parks

This Scandinavian-designed jungle gym (made by the Danish company KOMPAN) doesn't look like the usual playground setup, and it's not. Instead, the odd shapes in bright primary colors are meant for kids to experiment with and figure out. There's a pump for water play and a large climbing structure.

387 REESE'S RETREAT AT BROOKSIDE PARK

360 N Arroyo Blvd
Pasadena ⑬
+1 626 744 7311
ci.pasadena.ca.us/
PublicWorks/arroyo_
playgrounds

Located behind the Rose Bowl Aquatics Center (you can watch the high divers practice from here), this pirate-themed playground will have your little ones exclaiming, 'Shiver me timbers!'. The main play structure is a pirate ship with all kinds of climbing areas, a treasure hunt, and a sand-and-water area for younger children.

388 LOS ARBOLES ROCKETSHIP PARK

5101 Calle De Ricardo
Torrance ⑰
torranceca.gov/
22183.htm

The center of this playground at the 6-acre Los Arboles Park is a 28-foot-tall rocket ship that provides a spectacular view of the South Bay and is over half a century old. While the rest of the playground has been updated, it's wonderful that residents rallied to save this relic from the space age.

389 VINCENT LUGO PARK

Prospect Avenue
& Wells Street
San Gabriel ⑯
+1 626 308 2800
friendsoflalaguna.org

Children (and adults!) can slide down a giant snail or through the mouth of a pink whale at this cheerful playground affectionately known as the Dinosaur Park. Mexican artist Benjamin Dominguez created these 15 delightful concrete structures by hand in 1965, and today they are on the National Register of Historic Places.

390 MALIBU BLUFFS PARK

24250 Pacific Coast
Highway
Malibu ①
+1 310 317 1364
malibucity.org/facilities

Located on a 6-acre park that overlooks the Pacific Ocean, this playground is appropriately ocean-themed. Not only is there a whale structure to play on, there's a whale-watching station to see actual whales. Plus, there is a sand play area that steals attention away from the breathtaking view for a bit.

387 REESE'S RETREAT AT BROOKSIDE PARK

5 places to
GET WET

---

391 ANNENBERG COMMUNITY BEACH HOUSE

415 Pacific Coast Highway
Santa Monica ②
+1 310 458 4904
*annenberg
beachhouse.com*

There's reserved parking, a splash pad, a playground, a gorgeous, historic pool, and, of course, the beach – all at the Annenberg Community Beach House with no membership fees or purchase requirements. There's a small fee to use the pool, but the other amenities – including the all-important rest rooms – are free.

392 GRAND PARK

200 N Grand Avenue
Downtown ⑩
+1 213 972 8080
grandparkla.org

Trimmed by hot pink picnic tables and chairs, this park in the heart of downtown's civic center is an urban oasis. There's a fantastic playground for kids, and the splash pad at the restored Arthur J. Will Memorial Fountain is not only great fun, it makes for great photographs with City Hall in the background.

393 HANSEN DAM AQUATIC CENTER

11798 Foothill Blvd
Lake View Terrace/
San Fernando Valley ⑭
+1 818 899 3779
hansendam.
lacitypools.com

Visitors can fish or swim at this 40-acre recreation facility with a lake and a public pool. Open all summer, the pool has waterslides, sand surrounding it, and a grassy picnic area. If that's not enough water for you, take stand-up paddleboard lessons at the lake next door.

394 ROSE BOWL AQUATICS CENTER

360 N Arroyo Blvd
Pasadena ⑬
+1 626 564 0330
rosebowlaquatics.com

Located in Brookside Park (same place as the pirate-themed Reese's Retreat playground), this world-class aquatics facility has two Olympic pools that are open for public use. Be sure to check the website for family swim hours.

395 STONER PARK POOL

1835 Stoner Avenue
West LA ②
+1 310 575 8286
laparks.org/
reccenter/stoner

Open throughout the summer months, this public facility has a zero-entry wading pool with fun water features and fountains that will keep the kids cool and busy for hours. It's a wet wonderland for the kids, with a giant water slide that will delight daredevil kids of all ages.

5

KID ACTIVITIES
you'll find only in LA

---

396 AUTRY MUSEUM OF THE AMERICAN WEST

4700 Western
Heritage Way
Griffith Park ⑪
+1 323 667 2000
theautry.org

Located in Griffith Park, the Autry sponsors a host of family-friendly events to introduce their collections to the public. There's panning for gold, films projected on the lawn, and an event called 'Odd Nights at the Autry' that combines an outdoor market with crafts, food, games, and live music.

397 BOB BAKER MARIONETTE THEATER

1345 W 1st Street
Downtown ⑩
+1 213 250 9995
bobbakermarionette
theater.com

This is the oldest children's theater company in Los Angeles. Although visionary founder Bob Baker passed away in 2014, his team of talented puppeteers continues the magical marionette shows that he oversaw for 53 seasons (he made many of the marionettes you still see). This is a beloved institution for generations of Angelenos.

398 STAR ECO STATION

10101 Jefferson Blvd
Culver City ④
+1 310 842 8060
ecostation.org

For an incredible hands-on experience in ecology and environmentalism, check this place out – it's an environmental science museum, a wildlife rescue center, and a haven for exotic animals confiscated by the U.S. Fish and Wildlife Service. Kids can have up-close encounters with rescued animals from parrots to pythons.

399 KIDSPACE CHILDREN'S MUSEUM

480 N Arroyo Blvd
Pasadena ⑬
+1 626 449 9144
kidspacemuseum.org

There's plenty to engage kids ages one to ten at this exploratory museum, from a human-size weaving ant tunnel to the Imagination Workshop (where kids can make circuits and explore electronics). But the best features are outdoors – especially the Arroyo Adventure, where kids can explore a hawk's nest and play in the mud.

400 LOS ANGELES COUNTY MUSEUM OF ART (LACMA)

5905 Wilshire Blvd
Miracle Mile ⑧
+1 323 857 6000
lacma.org/kids-families

LACMA is a great place to take kids; they offer a free membership to children that also admits one adult. The outdoor sculptures 'Urban Lights' and 'Levitated Mass' are infinite fun to play in, and there's brush painting daily in the Boone Children's Gallery. Sundays are 'Family Days' with kid-friendly art projects.

5 great places to
PLAY IN
GRIFFITH PARK

---

401 MERRY-GO-ROUND

4730 Crystal
Springs Drive
Griffith Park ⑪
+1 323 665 3051
laparks.org/
griffithpark/griffith-
park-merry-go-round

Located between the LA Zoo and the
Los Feliz entrance, this 1926 treasure
has entertained five generations of
families from its quiet home in the park.
Reportedly, Walt Disney liked to bring
his children here and was inspired by the
carousel to create Disneyland.

402 SHANE'S INSPIRATION

4800 Crystal
Springs Drive
Griffith Park ⑪
+1 818 988 5676
shanesinspiration.org

Opened in 2000, this is the very first
universally accessible playground in
California. It was named in honor of Shane
Alexander Williams, a baby born with
spinal muscular atrophy, who passed away
two weeks after his birth. His parents and
other concerned citizens worked together
to make this inclusive playground possible.

403 LOS ANGELES ZOO AND BOTANICAL GARDENS

5333 Zoo Drive
Griffith Park ⑪
+1 323 644 4200
lazoo.org

If you take time to visit the grounds of the
Old Zoo also in Griffith Park, you'll see
the LA Zoo has come a long way. Today's
113-acre facility is home to more than
250 species of animals and 15 different
botanical collections. Its focus is animal
conservation and education.

404 PONIES & SOUTHERN RAILROAD

4400 Crystal
Springs Drive
Griffith Park ⑪
+1 323 664 3266 (pony)
+1 800 438 1297 (train)
griffithparkponyride.com
griffithparktrainrides.com

Gear up for some classic kiddie entertainment by wearing your cowboy hat or conductor's cap for this family-friendly fun. Operating in the park since 1948, these two attractions have been enjoyed by generations. Ponies are available in varying sizes and speeds, and the miniature train (built in the 1960s) travels a one-mile track.

405 TRAVEL TOWN

5200 Zoo Drive
Griffith Park ⑪
+1 323 662 5874
traveltown.org

There's more than one stop for the train-obsessed in Griffith Park and this is the granddaddy of them all – a collection of old train cars and steam engines that is both a transportation museum and a recreation center. Is there anything better than climbing on old train cars? Maybe riding the miniature one.

405 TRAVEL TOWN

SHORE HOTEL

30 PLACES
TO SLEEP

The 5 trendiest
HIPSTER
hotels

---

406 ACE HOTEL

929 S Broadway
Downtown ⑩
+1 213 623 3233
acehotel.com/losangeles

In 2014, the hip hotel came to LA by renovating the historic 13-floor United Artists building. Sleek but homey rooms offer an acoustic guitar or a record player with a selection of vinyl curated by Amoeba Music. Every night, the rooftop bar features DJs, bands, and more.

407 AVALON HOTEL

9400 W Olympic
Boulevard
Beverly Hills ⑤
+1 310 277 5221
avalon-hotel.com

This mid-century modern oasis offers a secluded escape in the middle of bustling Olympic Boulevard. Kelly Wearstler-designed rooms invite you to West Coast chill, and the stylish Viviane Restaurant features California cuisine. Of course, a 1950s-style cocktail in a poolside cabana is mandatory.

408 THE LINE HOTEL

3515 Wilshire Blvd
Koreatown ⑨
+1 213 381 7411
thelinehotel.com

Finally, a hotel as interesting as the neighborhood it's in and meant to inspire community. Stripped-down concrete-walled rooms with floor-to-ceiling windows and handmade furnishings reverberate artistic style and LA's casual, laidback culture. Chill by the pool or take in delectable offerings of food-truck pioneer chef Roy Choi.

409 HOTEL COVELL

4626 Hollywood Blvd
Los Feliz ⑦
+1 323 660 4300
hotelcovell.com

This five-room boutique hotel nestled above the Covell Wine Bar offers an upscale-yet-feels-like-home vibe. Order food from downstairs, watch the sunset from the rooftop deck, head downstairs to enjoy a variety of wine and beer, stumble upstairs to your room and put on a record, fall asleep. Wake up, repeat.

410 HOTEL ERWIN

1697 Pacific Avenue
Venice ③
+1 310 452 1111
hotelerwin.com

A Venice Beach destination since 1975, this cozy hotel is a block from the beach and the Venice Boardwalk. Watch the sun set over the Pacific from your 1970s funky fresh room, then hit the rooftop bar or have a quick bite with travelers from around the world at the Barlo Kitchen.

406 ACE HOTEL

5
HAUNTED
hotels

---

411 ALEXANDRIA HOTEL

501 S Spring Street
Downtown ⑩
+1 213 614 0152

Once a glitzy home to Chaplin and Valentino, the century-old Alexandria weathered decades of neglect and has now been revitalized. But the spirits never left – from the 9th floor 'ghost wing' to the haunted elevator that starts and stops on its own – or perhaps by the spirit hand of Valentino.

412 THE GEORGIAN

1415 Ocean Avenue
Santa Monica ②
+1 310 395 9945
georgianhotel.com

This posh 1933 Art Deco hotel at the end of Route 66 was once a luxury retreat for the rich and famous. It's now refurbished and landmarked, and the new elite enjoy the ocean view and imbibe at the speakeasy restaurant where employees claim to have seen apparitions and heard ghostly voices.

413 HOTEL FIGUEROA

939 S Figueroa Street
Downtown ⑩
+1 213 627 8971
hotelfigueroa.com

Flickering lights, elevators stopping on random floors, TVs turning off on their own, perhaps decades of earthquakes have loosened the wiring throughout this Moroccan-themed hotel, but many believe the spirit of Hallie Oswald roams the halls looking for her lover Harry Gordon – who murdered her there in 1950.

414 MILLENNIUM BILTMORE HOTEL

506 S Grand Avenue
Downtown ⑩
+1 213 624 1011
millenniumhotels.com

The glitz and glamour of the magnificent Biltmore remains (the basement pool is especially stunning). This early home to the Academy Awards ceremony was also the last place the Black Dahlia was seen before her gruesome murder. Sightings of a woman in black who vanishes add to the mystery of this unsolved case.

415 SITE OF CECIL HOTEL

640 S Main Street
Downtown ⑩

This mansion of murder and death was once home to Richard Ramirez, aka the Night Stalker. Within its seedy confines, many drug-addled and suicide-prone individuals found refuge along with the famous serial killer. For years, death followed many who entered and even the cops didn't want to darken the cursed doors.

412 THE GEORGIAN

5 hotels with
HISTORY

---

416 ANDAZ

8401 Sunset Blvd
West Hollywood ⑥
+1 323 656 1234
westhollywood.
andaz.hyatt.com

The former Hyatt (or Riot) House was the hotel of choice for 1970s rock 'n' rollers. From the Rolling Stones' Keith Richards throwing a TV out the window to Led Zeppelin renting out six floors and John Bonham riding his motorcycle through the lobby, the Riot House lived up to its moniker.

417 CHATEAU MARMONT

8221 Sunset Blvd
West Hollywood ⑥
+1 323 656 1010
chateaumarmont.com

Perched on a hill overlooking the Sunset Strip, the Chateau's secluded elegance has inspired generations of Hollywood creatives. From Fitzgerald to Sofia Coppola, Jim Morrison to James Franco, if the walls could talk they would tell many stories, and also sigh remembering John Belushi's 1982 overdose in Bungalow 3.

418 THE HOLLYWOOD ROOSEVELT

7000 Hollywood Blvd
Hollywood ⑦
+1 323 856 1970
thehollywood
roosevelt.com

Home to the first Academy Awards, the Roosevelt has been remodeled and revamped, but retains much of its Spanish Colonial Revival style, which Marilyn Monroe enjoyed over the two years she lived here. Party in the cabanas around David Hockney's painted pool or stroll down the heart of Hollywood Boulevard.

419 MAISON 140

140 S Lasky Drive
Beverly Hills ⑤
+1 310 281 4001
maison140.com

This former mansion was once the home to silent screen stars – and sisters – Lillian and Dorothy Gish (little-known fact: both directed films as well). Modernized with sexy design by Kelly Wearstler, the upscale retreat is steps from the boutiques of Rodeo Drive, offering a grown-up escape.

420 THE VENICE BEACH HOUSE

15 30th Avenue
Venice ③
+1 310 823 1966
venicebeachhouse.com

Not long after Abbot Kinney transformed acres of marshland into the Venice of America attraction, newspaper owner Warren Wilson decided to build a hotel on this white sand beach. In 1911 he opened the Venice Beach House as an antidote to city life. A century later the historic craftsman continues to offer a respite.

418 THE HOLLYWOOD ROOSEVELT

The 5 most
ECO-FRIENDLY
hotels

---

421 LOS FELIZ LODGE

1509 N Hoover Street
Los Feliz ⑦
+1 323 660 4150
losfelizlodge.com

A welcome alternative to the traditional hotel, here you will feel like a *La La Land* starlet in one of the cozy bungalows or villas. Each charming, bright room features a kitchen, bath, and plenty of space for family and friends. Stay a night or a month.

422 SHORE HOTEL

1515 Ocean Avenue
Santa Monica ②
+1 310 458 1515
shorehotel.com

This boutique hotel is enclosed by beautiful wood and glass – with clear ocean views even from the shower. The Shore Hotel is LEED Gold Certified, and a leader in offering luxury without waste – from the solar-heated pool, to the sustainable wood furniture to their partnership with Clean the World Foundation.

423 TERRANEA RESORT

100 Terranea Way
Rancho Palos Verdes ⑰
+1 866 547 3066
terranea.com

This Mediterranean-inspired escape – the only luxury eco-resort in the LA area – is situated on a 102-acre peninsula surrounded by the Pacific. The well-appointed bungalows, casitas, and villas are nestled between four pools, eight restaurants, spa facilities, and a golf course.

424 VENICE BEACH ECO COTTAGES

447 Grand Blvd
Venice ③
+1 866 802 3110
venicebeach
ecocottages.com

These three unique and cozy cottages offer a solar-powered green alternative to hotel life. You can live like a local just four blocks from the beach. Take your pick from the adorably themed cabins: the masculine Papa Hemingway, the 1940s-inspired Aunt Zoe's Place, or the 1960s Parisian Le Bébé Cottage.

425 WESTIN BONAVENTURE HOTEL & SUITES

404 S Figueroa St
Downtown ⑩
+1 213 624 1000
thebonaventure.com

This massive, luxury landmark has more than 1300 rooms – it's a true city within the city. As LA's first hotel to reach the environmental standards set by Green Seal, it's also lux with a conscious. Plus, you can take the *True Lies* elevator to the revolving bar on the top floor for a 360-degree view.

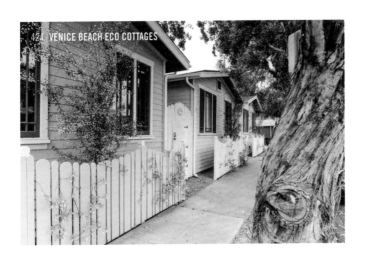

424 VENICE BEACH ECO COTTAGES

5
KITSCHY SPOTS
to sleep

---

426 THE CHARLIE HOTEL
819 N Sweetzer Ave
West Hollywood ⑥
+1 323 988 9000
thecharliehotel.com

Pay homage to the great star of the silent era in one of the 14 English-themed private bungalows here. Supposedly Chaplin himself lived here in the 1920s, and as the gorgeous California light streams in through large windows in your quaint bungalow, you might feel inspired to write a screenplay.

427 FARMER'S DAUGHTER
115 S Fairfax Avenue
Fairfax ⑧
+1 323 937 3930
farmersdaughter
hotel.com

This 1960s-styled boutique hotel offers an artistic home away from home, with each room presenting a unique depiction of the eponymous character. Located across the street from the iconic Farmers' Market, it's walking distance to numerous restaurants, cafes, bars, and more.

428 MAGIC CASTLE HOTEL
7025 Franklin Ave
Hollywood ⑦
+1 323 851 0800
magiccastlehotel.com

Nestled in the Hollywood Hills, this 1960 former apartment building now offers rooms with kitchenettes and a quaint pool with the best service in town – free popsicles and snacks. Plus, the best perk: access to the exclusive Magic Castle.

429 SAFARI INN

1911 W Olive Avenue
Burbank ⑭
+1 818 845 8586
coastanabelle.com/
safari

With its original 1950s décor and iconic neon sign, this landmark two-story motor inn has retained its vintage charm. A much-used location for TV and film, including *True Romance*, *Apollo 13*, and *CSI*. Channel your inner Tarantino in the simple rooms or chill by the pool.

430 THE QUEEN MARY

1126 Queens Highway
Long Beach ⑰
+1 877 342 0738
queenmary.com

Permanently docked in Long Beach since 1967, this once grand Cunard ocean liner is now a floating hotel. The stately Art Deco marvel features large suites and over 300 pristine staterooms. Unwind with a walk around the deck, enjoy fine dining and boutiques, and relax at the spa – all aboard!

427 FARMER'S DAUGHTER

5 hotels
TO HEAR
THE OCEAN

431 CADILLAC HOTEL

8 Dudley Avenue
Venice ③
+1 310 399 8876
thecadillachotel.com

Situated right on the bustling boardwalk, this 1914 landmark once drew the likes of Chaplin, Jim Morrison, and Janis Joplin and continues to attract artists and travelers looking for a perfect oceanside spot to enjoy the bohemian offerings of Venice.

432 FAIRMONT MIRAMAR HOTEL & BUNGALOWS

101 Wilshire Blvd
Santa Monica ②
+1 310 576 7777
fairmont.com

Perched on bluffs overlooking the Pacific, this roaring 20s landmark has drawn many celebrities and politicians, from Greta Garbo to John F. Kennedy, Steven Spielberg, and President Clinton. This exclusive retreat is also a Green Certified hotel, and offers 32 bungalows and 302 stylish rooms.

433 BEACH HOUSE – HERMOSA BEACH

1300 The Strand
Hermosa Beach ⑰
+1 310 374 3001
beach-house.com

Though it's ten minutes from LAX, this hotel feels closer to a New England beach cottage than a United Airlines hub. Directly outside the light-filled studios is the famous 23-mile bike path that you should certainly take advantage of – plus complimentary yoga and pilates on the beach.

434 THE PORTOFINO HOTEL & MARINA

260 Portofino Way
Redondo Beach ⑰
+1 310 379 8481
hotelportofino.com

Opened in 1965 by Mary Davis, a racecar driver and Hollywood stunt driver, this hotel gained notoriety in the 1970s for being the finish line of the coast-to-coast race that inspired *The Gumball Rally*. Today the hotel epitomizes nautical chic with plenty of seaside activities to check out: sea lions, bike riding, paddle boarding.

435 MALIBU BEACH INN

22878 Pacific Coast Highway
Malibu ①
+1 800 462 5428
malibubeachinn.com

This roadside motel was rehabbed into a luxurious and opulent boutique hotel – every room has a private balcony and faces the water. The hotel has access to the most exclusive piece of Malibu's beach, nicknamed 'Billionaire's Beach'. It's also walking distance to the Malibu Pier and the Malibu County Mart.

435 MALIBU BEACH INN

431 CADILLAC HOTEL

JOSHUA TREE NATIONAL PARK

35 WEEKEND GETAWAYS

---

5 top
DESERT DESTINATIONS

---

436 DEATH VALLEY
nps.gov/deva/index.htm

Not a trip for the faint of heart or a summertime destination, Death Valley is the biggest US National Park outside of Alaska and a 200-mile, scenic trip from LA. There's 3,4 million acres of wild country out here to explore, from barren salt flats to rugged mountains. Make plans and bring water.

437 JOSHUA TREE NATIONAL PARK
nps.gov/jotr/index.htm

For a magical desert experience closer to LA, this national park with its namesake twisted trees is a study in stark beauty. It's a great place to camp and hike – or if you'd rather stay in a hotel, try the charming Joshua Tree Inn, where singer Gram Parsons passed.

438 LANDERS
yucca-valley.org/visitors

Located in the southeastern Mojave Desert, just north of Joshua Tree, is this desert community. Landers is less visited than other Yucca Valley desert communities. Far-out attractions include Giant Rock, a seven-story-high freestanding boulder (the largest in the world) and the Integratron, the ultimate place for a sound bath.

439 LAS VEGAS

lvcva.com

It's Vegas, baby! What more is there to say? This: you might be tempted to try to road-trip this – unless you've got plenty of time, don't. It's much faster (and sometimes less expensive) to fly from LAX or Burbank.

440 PALM SPRINGS

visitpalmsprings.com

Go for a vintage getaway to this celebrated desert oasis – a mere two-hour drive from Los Angeles, there's lots to see here (The Living Desert Museum, Palm Springs Aerial Tramway), but the best way to holiday is a mid-century hotel with a pool.

440 PALM SPRINGS

436 DEATH VALLEY

5 *enchanting*
SNOWY LOCALES

---

441 BIG BEAR LAKE

bigbear.com

It's true that in LA you can surf at the beach in the morning and ski on a mountain later that afternoon. Located in the San Bernardino Mountains and less than 100 miles from LA, Big Bear boasts Southern California's largest recreational lake and in winter the area is a popular destination for skiing and snowboarding.

442 LAKE ARROWHEAD

lakearrowhead.com

Also in the San Bernardino Mountains, Arrowhead is even closer to LA than Big Bear – a mere 80 miles. And like Big Bear, it's a popular winter resort for skiing but is just as lovely in the summer and spring, when the cooler temperatures provide relief from the hot city below.

443 IDYLLWILD
idyllwild.com

The quaint community, nestled into the San Jacinto mountains, is home to adorable A-frame homes and wooden cabins hidden in the pines. There's fresh air, hiking, rock climbing on Tahquitz Peak, a village of mom-and-pop shops, and not much else. The perfect place for a getaway that includes board games.

444 MOUNT BALDY
mtbaldy.com

From LA, it takes less than two hours to get to the highest peak in the San Gabriel Mountains. In the winter, there is skiing, but in the summer the 1950s ski lift runs for hikers and those seeking the respite of the Top of the Notch restaurant with its epic views of Angeles National Forest.

445 WRIGHTWOOD
*wrightwood
mountainresort.com*

Just 90 minutes away from LA, this idyllic town in the Angeles National Forest has the closest winter resort available, called Mountain High. During ski season there's even a 'Rally Bus', which for 40 dollars will pick you up in LA and deliver you mountainside.

5 fun
BEACH-BOUND
trips

446 BALBOA ISLAND
balboaisland.com

A mere 45 miles from LA, this man-made island in Newport Beach is a sunny bit of seaside heaven. It's charming and quaint and the real estate is some of the most expensive in the US. *Arrested Development* fans will recognize this as the site of the Bluth's frozen banana stand.

447 CATALINA ISLAND
catalinachamber.com

Because it's accessible only by sea or by air (easier than it sounds, there are four mainland ports with ferries), Catalina feels much further away than it really is. Maybe that's because once you arrive you are on 'island time', with no cars (rent a taxi, bike or golf cart) and plenty of leisure activities.

448 MORRO BAY
morrobay.org

Just three hours up the coast from LA, getting to Morro Bay is half the fun – the drive, up the 101 or on the Pacific Coast Highway, is beautiful. Once you get to the sleepy little beach town, you'll be happy to finally dive into the Pacific.

449 **LAGUNA BEACH**
visitlagunabeach.com

Only 50 miles south of Los Angeles, this tiny beach community boasts many galleries, cafes, and boutiques. There are also great hikes to secluded coves and a plethora of tide pools. The area is an 'artist colony', but nowadays the real estate is so expensive, few artists can actually afford to live here.

450 **CORONADO**
*coronado
visitorcenter.com*

This resort city across the San Diego Bay has some of the best beaches in the US. Another reason to come is the historic Hotel del Coronado, a national landmark that has hosted distinguished guests (most US presidents, Muhammad Ali, Marilyn Monroe) and might have inspired author L. Frank Baum's *Emerald City*.

449 LAGUNA BEACH

5
FOLK ART
wonders

---

451 BEASTS BY RICARDO BRECEDA

3759–4167 Borrego
Springs Road
Borrego Springs
*borregosprings
chamber.com*

This isolated community sits in the
midst of the incredible Anza-Borrego
Desert State Park, and on a nearby parcel
of land known as the Galleta Meadows
are more than 100 large-scale metal
sculptures by artist Ricardo Breceda.
If the surroundings didn't astonish enough,
try adding dinosaurs, dragons, and giant
grasshoppers to the desert landscape.

452 SALVATION MOUNTAIN

Beal Road
Niland
*bob@
salvationmountain.us*
salvationmountain.us

Near Niland (about a three-hour drive
from LA, an hour and a half from Palm
Springs) lies an awesome site: a towering
clay mountain resplendent with life –
colorful paintings of flowers, trees, and
birds. It was created in 1984 by artist
Leonard Knight, who painted his message
– as well as other scriptures – atop:
'God is Love'.

453 EAST JESUS

East Jesus Road
Slab City
eastjesus.org

Less than a mile away from Salvation Mountain, East Jesus is an experimental, sustainable, educational art installation and community. Known as 'the last free place', East Jesus is off the grid, with no municipal utility services, and the artists who live there are charged with maintaining and protecting the 'collaborative canvas'.

454 GRANDMA PRISBREY'S BOTTLE VILLAGE

4595 Cochran Street
Simi Valley
+1 805 231 2947
bottlevillage.com

In the midst of staid Simi Valley is this wonderland of refuse and historic landmark. The work of a self-taught senior citizen, Bottle Village is a ⅓-acre site with structures, wishing wells, and mosaic walks all made from discarded glass bottles. Check the website for information about upcoming tours.

455 MADONNA INN

100 Madonna Road
San Luis Obispo
+1 805 543 3000
madonnainn.com

San Luis Obispo is a wonderful town, but you might not see much of it because you'll be too busy exploring this wonderfully wacky and historic motor inn. The vision of Alex and Phyllis Madonna, the building itself makes ample use of native stone and rock, and each of the 110 guest rooms has a different theme for its décor.

The 5 most beautiful
COUNTRY ESCAPES

456 BAKERSFIELD

visitbakersfield.com

Bakersfield is a big city – not really a country escape – but you are here to pay homage to the famous Bakersfield sound, a genre of country music created in honky-tonks here in the 1950s. Some famous practitioners were Buck Owens, Merle Haggard, and Jean Shepard.

457 LOS ALAMOS

visitsyv.com/discover-syv/los-alamos

Located 140 miles from LA, this small town is the 'entry' into Santa Ynez Valley, and is surrounded by vineyards, ranches, and farms. It's a good place to get a taste of the Old West – there are Victorian-era buildings and hotels in town and lots of ranches outside of town that will rent you a horse.

458 OAK GLEN

oakglen.net

A mere 80 miles from LA, this is apple country. Due to its elevation, the cooler climate (it even snows in the winter) permits a plethora of apple orchards in the area, many of which offer pick-your-own explorations. So take the family for a wholesome experience, plus homemade apple pie and freshly pressed cider.

459 **SOLVANG**

solvangusa.com

If you thought it unlikely to find a Danish village in the midst of Santa Barbara wine country, think again. *'Solvang'* is Danish for 'sunny field', which is what the Danes discovered when they settled here in 1911. Today, the town is popular with tourists who come to enjoy the exotic architecture and bakeries.

460 **VENTURA**

visitventuraca.com

This coastal town only about an hour's drive north of LA is home to the Channel Islands National Park and Marine Sanctuary, a series of five islands where there are no hotels (camping is permitted), cell service, or running water. The islands are only accessible by boat or plane with prior reservations.

460 **VENTURA**

5 tasty
WINE TOURS

---

461 LOS OLIVOS
losolivosca.com

Named for a nearby olive ranch, this historic town is high on the charm factor: tree-lined streets of Victorian homes in town and horse ranches and vineyards in the surrounding area. There are dozens of nearby tasting rooms, most with expansive views of the Santa Ynez Valley.

462 OJAI
ojaivisitors.com

This mystical mountain town is proud of what locals call 'the pink moment', at dusk when the entire Ojai Valley turns into a palate of pink tones. It's breathtaking and worth the two-hour drive from LA for that alone. But there's also wine from the nearby vineyards and fresh produce from orchards.

463 **PASO ROBLES**
pasowine.com

One of the wonderful things about Southern and Central Coastal vineyards is they aren't Napa; vintners here are still funky and unpretentious about their wines, even though many of them are top-notch in terms of quality. Paso Robles epitomizes the laidback vibe even though it's the fastest-growing wine-producing area in California.

464 **SANTA BARBARA**
santabarbaraca.com

The standard for weekend getaways from LA, this gorgeous beach town on what's called the American Riviera has everything: beaches, history, wine. It also has La Super-Rica Taqueria, a roadside Mexican stand that Julia Child often cited as her favorite restaurant – and that is reason enough for a road trip.

465 **TEMECULA**
visittemeculavalley.com

About 90 miles southeast of Los Angeles, this area has been called the new Napa thanks to its sophisticated wines and bucolic landscape. The Temecula Valley has been the center of Southern California's wine making since the 1960s, when vintners Mount Palomar and Callaway first started. Today there are more than 40 wineries.

The 5 top
TRAIN TRIPS

---

466 GOLETA
gogoleta.com

A two-and-a-half-hour train ride up the Pacific coast will land you at this laidback beach town just north of Santa Barbara. If gardens are your thing, there are plenty of them. There's also the Goleta Butterfly Grove. Plus, the beautiful Goleta County Beach.

467 RIVERSIDE
riversidecvb.com

From Union Station, the Metrolink commuter train travels to this vibrant city in the Inland Empire. Visit the incredible Spanish Mission-style Mission Inn Hotel and Spa, a national historic landmark from the early 1900s. Wealthy travelers came from around the world to stay here, and Hollywood loved to use the stunning hotel as a setting for films.

468 SAN CLEMENTE
sanclementeguide.com

Halfway between LA and San Diego, the ride to San Clemente on Amtrak's Pacific Surfliner is pretty much the perfect rail trip – it's less than two hours and packed full of incredible views of the Pacific. Plus the train station is walking distance to downtown San Clemente, so you don't need a car.

469 SAN DIEGO

sandiego.org

It's only a two-hour car drive from LA to San Diego – provided there's no traffic. There's *always* traffic, so take the train instead, and in roughly the same amount of time you will arrive at the seaside city with its wealth of attractions refreshed and relaxed instead of full of freeway rage.

470 SAN LUIS OBISPO

visitslo.com

For a real rail adventure, this six-hour ride up the coast on Amtrak's Pacific Surfliner route will give you unspoiled views of the California coast. At the end of the line is this popular resort town, and many of the nicer hotels offer complimentary bicycles that you can use to get around (or rent one).

469 SAN DIEGO

30 RANDOM FACTS & DETAILS

The 5 best dystopic NOVELS ABOUT HOLLYWOOD

---

471 APE AND ESSENCE
BY ALDOUS HUXLEY
1948

Published in 1948, this novel is both a satire of Hollywood and a vision of a dystopic world, where humans have become apes that destroy themselves. The novel structure is interesting: two film-industry exes go to the desert (where Huxley lived at the time of writing) in search of a screenwriter; that man's screenplay composes most of the novel.

472 THE DAY OF THE LOCUST
BY NATHANAEL WEST
1939

West's novel is a scathing critique of the American dream set among the biggest proponents of it – the health seekers and Hollywood strivers of Los Angeles. The protagonist is a newly arrived set designer living in Hollywood; many of his experiences derive from West's own life – working as screenwriter, he lived in a hotel on Hollywood Boulevard.

473 LESS THAN ZERO
BY BRET EASTON ELLIS
1985

This 1985 novel about morally vacuous teenagers in LA was also made into the 1987 film starring Robert Downey Jr. It follows the main character, Clay, who has returned home to LA after his first semester in college to find much hedonism and casual nihilism among his over-privileged friends.

474 PLAY IT AS IT LAYS
BY JOAN DIDION
1970

The bard of California, Didion offers incredible insights into life on the left coast, but her 1970 novel about a washed-up actress and her estranged Hollywood-director husband captured the ennui, not just of the Hollywood elite, but of American society.

475 WHAT MAKES SAMMY RUN?
BY BUDD SCHULBERG
1941

Often cited as the best book about the dark side of Hollywood, this is the book all aspiring actors should read. The novel follows Sammy Glick, a poor Jewish kid from New York, as he rises, unscrupulously, to Hollywood power. Schulberg wrote what he knew – he was an acclaimed screenwriter, and his father ran a film studio.

5

LA DISASTER FILMS

476 **2012**
2009

No city is destroyed more in the movies than LA. In this 2009 film directed by Roland Emmerich, a cataclysmic earthquake destroys the city while John Cusack's character, a limo driver/novelist, escapes with his family in a plane. LA's freeways are uprooted like weeds, its downtown skyline collapses, and Santa Monica and other beach cities fall into the Pacific.

477 **INDEPENDENCE DAY**
1996

This 1996 film about an alien invasion, also directed by Roland Emmerich, features a great sequence where downtown's U.S. Bank Building is obliterated by a flying saucer that hits it with a laser.

478 TERMINATOR 2: JUDGMENT DAY
1991

In this 1991 sequel, character Sarah Connor has a vision of the nuclear apocalypse that will destroy the world – but first it destroys Los Angeles while she watches. A playground with a wide view of the downtown skyline is the setting – the people, like the palm trees, are blown sideways, catch on fire, and turn to dust.

479 VOLCANO
1997

In a bit of questionable science, a small earthquake provokes a deadly volcano that in the 1997 film erupts in the La Brea Tar Pits. Lava flows down Wilshire Boulevard, destroying landmarks like Johnie's Coffee Shop and entering the Metro Red Line before the hero diverts the flow into the Pacific.

480 WAR OF THE WORLDS
1953

The cinematic destruction of Los Angeles started early, as evidenced in the 1953 version of *War of the Worlds*. Invading Martians attack the city, blowing up City Hall (a model, of course) in Technicolor.

5

WILDLIFE SPECIES

to watch out for

---

481 BLACK WIDOW SPIDER

Few other large cities are home to such a diverse population of wildlife – the key to coexistence is to give the animals respect and space. Black Widow spiders, which have toxic (although usually not fatal) bites, are native to the area, so be sure to check beneath patio furniture and park benches.

482 COYOTES

No matter where you are in LA – even in dense areas downtown. You might hear or see a coyote. They thrive near urban areas thanks to the bountiful amounts of trash and fallen fruit from trees. Experts suggest you keep a distance (but don't run) and 'haze' the animal by making loud noises and waving your arms.

483 MOUNTAIN LIONS

Though there are a few of them living in the nearby mountain ranges (and one, named P-22, living in Griffith Park), it's highly unlikely you will see a mountain lion while hiking in even the most remote of LA's parks – they are nocturnal, and it's their nature to avoid people.

484 MOSQUITOES

We love our water features in Los Angeles – fountains, ponds, and pools. But neglected or improperly kept, bodies of stagnant water draw mosquitoes, some of which carry diseases like the West Nile virus. For that reason, be sure to get rid of any standing water around your residence.

485 RATTLESNAKES

While a mountain lion sighting is unlikely while hiking LA's miles of remote trails, it's not unlikely to come upon a rattlesnake sunning itself alongside a trail, so always be aware of where you are putting your hands and feet and stay on the trails.

5 *useful bits of*
FREEWAY LINGO

486 HOV LANES

'HOV' stands for High Occupancy Vehicle – 2 or more people riding in it – and in LA there's a whole HOV system to ease traffic congestion and incentivize ride sharing. Special lanes (also called 'diamond' lanes) and on-ramps are designated 'HOV', so that travelers who carpool have more reliable travel.

487 PCH

By this stage of the book, you've likely spent some time on 'PCH', or Pacific Coast Highway, the famed coastal highway known for its scenic views and occasional landslides. Part of the larger State Route 1, the section designated as PCH spans from Dana Point to Oxnard.

488 ROUND ROBIN

Don't mistake this maneuver for a police chase – sometimes California Highway Patrol motorcyclists or patrol cars zigzag across lanes of cars from left to right in a move called a 'round robin'. The purpose of the pattern is to slow down motorists behind the patrol person because of hazards in the road ahead.

489 SIGALERT

Often said on the radio in a traffic report, 'SigAlert' means there's a traffic jam or other problem on the freeway. Though many think it stands for cigarette break, the term derives from radio-station owner Loyd Sigmon, who had the idea to work with the LAPD to broadcast traffic problems.

490 'THE' BEFORE FREEWAY NUMBER

Perhaps the most distinctive feature of regional speech in Southern California is the practice of putting the definite article 'the' before the names of freeways. This practice gets big laughs on a recurring sketch on *Saturday Night Live* called 'The Californians', and mock it as you might, you'll find it habit-forming.

5
RADIO STATIONS
to tune in to

---

491 KCRW (89.9 FM)
kcrw.com

A National Public Radio member station, this beloved station operates from the campus of Santa Monica College. It plays original news and music programming plus NPR programs and affiliates. The morning music program, 'Morning Becomes Eclectic', is highly influential.

492 KLAX (97.9 FM)
klaxfm.radio.net

This Spanish-language station is one of LA's top-rated radio stations – its morning show beats out Howard Stern in terms of listeners. The music is contemporary *ranchera* music, which makes a great backdrop for driving around the city.

493 KPCC (89.3 FM)
scpr.org

Another National Public Radio member station, this Pasadena station is all talk radio and has fantastic original programs that focus on LA. The news department is among the most honored in Southern California radio.

494 KROQ (106.7 FM)
kroq.cbslocal.com

Known as the world-famous 'kay-rock', this commercial rock station was the 40-year home of DJ Rodney Bingenheimer, whose influential show introduced punk rock to mainstream success. The station also helped launch the careers of SoCal bands such as the Red Hot Chili Peppers, No Doubt, and Rage Against the Machine.

495 KXLU (88.9 FM)
kxlu.com

This non-commercial college radio station is broadcast from the Westchester campus of Loyola Marymount University and offers an eclectic range of programming. Music is a diverse mix of genres, including the show 'Alma Del Barrio', one of the longest-running Latin radio programs in the country.

5 ways to cross town during
RUSH HOUR

---

496 FOUNTAIN AVENUE

A famous anecdote that's attributed to Bette Davis is that a reporter once asked the Hollywood veteran for her advice for aspiring actors trying to make it in Hollywood and Davis wryly replied: "Take Fountain". It's true that Fountain Avenue moves faster through Hollywood than neighboring Santa Monica Boulevard.

497 LA CIENEGA BLVD TO LAX

Sometimes (like, say, during rush-hour traffic) it's better to avoid the freeways altogether and take the surface streets to the airport. When traveling from downtown, Hollywood, or West Hollywood, there are not-so-secret routes available along La Cienega Boulevard and La Brea Avenue.

498 SEPULVEDA BLVD INSTEAD OF THE 405 FREEWAY

Driving to and from the San Fernando Valley from the Westside means traveling through the Sepulveda Pass, the pass through the Santa Monica Mountains that links the LA basin to the Valley. There are two ways to do so: on the 405 freeway or via Sepulveda. Go with the latter.

499 OLYMPIC BLVD INSTEAD OF THE 10 FREEWAY

Getting from east to west and vice versa in Los Angeles is tough at almost any time (the middle of the night is best), but there are a number of surface streets to try during rush hour, including Olympic Boulevard – it was once 10th Street but was renamed in honor of the 1932 Olympics.

500 VENICE BLVD INSTEAD OF THE 10 FREEWAY

Another good option for getting to and from downtown and Santa Monica is Venice Boulevard, since the 10 freeway is usually a mess during popular commute times. A general rule: if you can, steer clear of freeways on Thursday and Friday evenings, which are peak traffic times.

INDEX

COLOPHON

EDITING *and* COMPOSING – Andrea Richards

GRAPHIC DESIGN – Joke Gossé, Sarah Schrauwen and Sarah Vanbelle

PHOTOGRAPHY – Giovanni Simeone – www.simephoto.com

COVER IMAGE – Mariachi Plaza Station (secret 293)

The addresses in this book have been selected after thorough independent research by the author, in collaboration with Luster Publishers. The selection is solely based on personal evaluation of the business by the author. Nothing in this book was published in exchange for payment or benefits of any kind.

D/2017/12.005/8
ISBN 978 94 6058 2073
NUR 510, 513

© 2017, Luster, Antwerp
www.lusterweb.com – www.the500hiddensecrets.com
info@lusterweb.com

Printed in Italy by Printer Trento.